HEALTHY GUT, FLAT STOMACH

ALSO BY DANIELLE CAPALINO

Healthy Gut, Flat Stomach Drinks

HEALTHY GUT, FLAT STOMACH

THE FAST AND EASY LOW-FODMAP DIET PLAN

Danielle Capalino, MSPH, RD

THE COUNTRYMAN PRESS
A division of W. W. Norton & Company
Independent Publishers Since 1923

NOTE

The information in this book is not intended to provide medical advice or to diagnose or treat medical diseases. It is strictly for informational purposes. Before undertaking any course of treatment, you should seek the advice of a doctor or health-care provider. I strongly encourage working with a dietitian who is trained in the low-FODMAP diet. If you are experiencing consistent or severe GI symptoms, you should first seek out medical attention to rule out other diagnoses.

If you are experiencing bleeding, symptoms that wake you up from sleep at night, symptoms that have changed dramatically or started suddenly, have had unintentional weight loss of more than 10 pounds, fever, or have a strong family history of colon cancer, seek the counsel of a medical professional before you embark on this diet plan.

All the information provided in this book regarding FODMAP content of foods is based on research that has been conducted at Monash University. All the information is accurate at the time of writing, but is subject to change as this is an emerging field. The recipes I have included use low-FODMAP ingredients, but have not been tested in a laboratory setting.

For information about permission to reproduce selections from this book, write to Permissions, The Countryman Press, 500 Fifth Avenue, New York, NY 10110

For information about special discounts for bulk purchases, please contact W. W. Norton Special Sales at specialsales@wwnorton.com or 800-233-4830
Manufacturing by Versa Press
Book design by Anna Reich
Production manager: Devon Zahn

Library of Congress Cataloging-in-Publication Data

Names: Capalino, Danielle, author.
Title: Healthy gut, flat stomach : the fast and easy low-FODMAP diet plan / Danielle Capalino, MSPH, RD.
Description: New York, NY : Countryman Press, a division of W.W. Norton & Company Independent Publishers Since 1923, [2017] | Includes bibliographical references and index.
Identifiers: LCCN 2016044942 | ISBN 9781581574142 (pbk.)
Subjects: LCSH: Gastrointestinal system—Diseases—Nutritional aspects—Popular works. | Gastrointestinal system—Diseases—Diet therapy—Recipes.
Classification: LCC RC806 .C37 2017 | DDC 641.5/63—dc23
LC record available at https://lccn.loc.gov/2016044942

The Countryman Press
www.countrymanpress.com

A division of W. W. Norton & Company, Inc.
500 Fifth Avenue, New York, NY 10110
www.wwnorton.com

978-1-58157-414-2 (pbk.)

10 9 8

CONTENTS

INTRODUCTION

Digestive woes are incredibly common. Up to one in five people suffer from these issues—everything from gas to constipation, bloating to stomachaches. Trying to figure out the cause can be so difficult that you give up in frustration. Most of the time the doctor doesn't even know what to tell you to do. Maybe you drink a tea that your mother suggested, or take a probiotic supplement you read about online. Or you may think you are sensitive to gluten. Sometimes you feel that you might be lactose intolerant, but other days you aren't sure.

Well, if you think it has something to do with what you're eating, you're probably right. The good news is that there actually is a scientifically proven, research-based diet that will reduce the bloat and alleviate uncomfortable abdominal symptoms. It has worked for a number of my patients, and it will work for you. I'm going to show you how, step by step, to determine what foods bother your gut, and help you create a personalized program of eating that makes you feel—and look—great.

I'm a nutritionist with a private practice in Manhattan, and I've carved out a space teaching this groundbreaking approach to food to my patients. I wish I had a better name for it, but it's known as the low-FODMAP diet.

The F-what diet? I'm sorry, I didn't invent the name. I don't really like it, either, but it's making its mark in the medical field and we should keep using it so everyone is on the same page. FODMAP is actually an acronym for a group of carbohydrates that are also impossible to pronounce or remember—but all of which have the potential to wreak havoc on your gut:

Fermentable
Oligosaccharides
Disaccharides
Monosaccharides
and
Polyols

Because they are broken down so slowly, these short chain carbohydrates (or sugars—*saccharide* means sugar, and sugar is built out of carbohydrates) are poorly absorbed in the small intestine. While they are hanging out in your gut, they act as fast food for the healthy bacteria that live there. What I mean by this is that healthy bacteria—which we want to nourish—break down these sugars, producing hydrogen, carbon dioxide, and methane gases, which cause bloating and discomfort.

While everyone has a hard time digesting these foods, some individuals are more sensitive than others and as a result can experience a slew of gastroenterological symptoms, such as gas, bloating, diarrhea, and constipation. This is especially true in the millions of people with irritable bowel syndrome (IBS—more on that later) and those with food intolerances and other digestive diseases. Studies show that up to 75 percent of IBS sufferers find relief when following a low-FODMAP diet.

FODMAPs are not bad for you; they are foods that you were eating before and many of them are actually very healthy! So, why should you stop eating them—at least temporarily? Because, although these foods can be packed with nutrients, they can also cause uncomfortable symptoms in your gut. The only way to figure out which foods are causing you trouble is to remove all of them from your diet and then reintroduce them one by one to find out which are to blame.

The foods that fall into each of the FODMAP categories are not very intuitive, so you do have to pay close attention to the lists I provide—and I make it as straightforward as possible. Once you get the hang of it and know what to do on your own, you will be able to use this book as an occasional reference.

FODMAPs are not necessarily bad for you; many of them are actually very healthy.

One of the best things about this book is that you are going to end up with a diet that is *personalized* for you. You read that right: not everyone who reads this book needs to follow the same exact diet, but the same approach will help you identify your personal triggers and charge forward with a diet that works for you, and makes you look and feel great.

In the pages that follow I am going to:

- Explain what the low-FODMAP diet is and why it is useful
- Provide you with an elimination diet and the tools you need to test which foods give you the most trouble
- Share great-tasting, simple recipes that are low in FODMAPs
- Give you strategies for eating out and grocery shopping

Before I get to the nitty-gritty, let me tell you about me, and why I want to be your partner through this life-changing diet plan.

MY STORY

Why did I decide to focus my practice on digestive health? When you are superpassionate about nutrition, it makes sense to look at the core—to ask, "Where does food go?" The answer, of course, is, "To your gut."

I love to feel empowered by making choices to make myself feel better. I have a history of severe joint problems and inflammation. When I was 23 years old, I started seeing doctor after doctor to address severe shoulder pain. After months of seeing specialists, an MRI revealed that my cartilage had completely degenerated, and no one knew why it happened. After consulting with several surgeons—most of whom believed I was too young for it—I underwent a total shoulder replacement. Going through a big surgery like a joint replacement—and having a scientific background—I was hungry to learn more about why this happened to me and what I could do to prevent this from happening to my other joints. I was not getting any answers from the doctors, and I kept wondering whether what I ate could make a difference to my physical health. My personal experience set me off on a journey to learn everything that I could about the deep connection between food and health.

At first, this journey meant buying a stack of books and reading about how diet affects inflammation. I quickly realized I wanted more than to just read a book—I wanted rigorous scientific knowledge on nutrition. I had been exposed to nutrition research as an undergraduate at MIT when I participated in research investigating the effects of carbohydrates on weight loss and seasonal affective disorder, so I already knew how intensely the power of what people eat can affect how they feel.

I was fortunate to continue my studies in nutrition at Johns Hopkins Bloomberg School of Public Health. Before I even moved to Baltimore, I researched the practitioners in the area and learned about Dr. Gerard Mullin. Dr. Mullin is an amazing doctor and human, a pioneer in gastroenterology and nutrition, and the author of several books on the topic of gut health. He is unique in his approach as a gastroenterologist, using food and nutrition in well-being and symptom management. I had the amazing experience of sitting alongside Dr. Mullin and his patients as they combatted various gastrointestinal (GI) ailments. It was in this setting in 2011 that I first learned about the low-FODMAP diet and got to see the dramatic effect it has on people's lives.

At Johns Hopkins we saw what I then thought was a surprising number of patients with gas and bloating who were suffering from IBS. They had tried and failed to get relief from medications—and were willing to try anything. Dr. Mullin pulled out a handout from his drawer and insisted that these patients work with a dietitian to try the low-FODMAP diet before they came back to see him. As part of my training, I shadowed a dietitian and so had a chance to see the same patients in a nutrition counseling setting. It changed my life course to see how significant the effect that this diet had on so many lives.

Dietitian vs. Nutritionist

Anyone can call him- or herself a nutritionist since the term is unregulated. A registered dietitian (RD, or dietitian for short) is a nutrition expert who has fulfilled undergraduate or graduate coursework in physiology and nutrition sciences; completed a 900-hour, supervised, hands-on internship; passed a comprehensive exam; and fulfills continuing education requirements set forth by the Academy of Nutrition and Dietetics.

After graduating from Johns Hopkins, I moved back to my hometown of New York City in 2013 and opened up my own practice. The low-FODMAP diet is still new and most dietitians are not trained in how to implement it, so it was a natural progression for me to establish myself as an expert in this space. I feel proud knowing that I offer my patients something that is research-based, highly effective, and unknown by most people in my field. I have counseled hundreds of patients on low-FODMAP living—and honed my skills teaching it so that I can teach you in this book, the same way I instruct my patients.

Do I follow this diet? The answer is yes; I have used the elimination diet as a tool to identify what was bloating my abdomen. A few years ago, I started feeling really terrible after meals—and sometimes I looked four months pregnant (which is shockingly common), and not from overeating. Then, I started waking up

looking completely distended as well. Luckily I had the tools in my back pocket and knew exactly how to treat myself. I went to my doctor first to rule out other possible conditions, such as celiac disease (more on this later), but he suggested—you guessed it—a low-FODMAP diet, and who better to go on the diet than me!

It really was not until I started the low-FODMAP diet that I returned to my normal unbloated self. I initially stayed on the elimination phase for two weeks, but I noticed such a big difference in how I looked and felt that I stayed on it (a little more liberally) for another two weeks before I started testing the foods that might be bothering me. When I say I followed the diet liberally, I mean I avoided obvious high-FODMAP foods such as apples, pears, beans, and milk—but I would go to a cocktail party and eat things that seemed low-FODMAP without checking on specific ingredients with a waiter.

Spoiler alert: I learned that in my case I can't eat onions and larger portions of bread. Or, rather, I *can* eat them, and sometimes I do, because I love onions, but I know I will suffer the consequences. Now, however, I am empowered with information and I know it is within my control to take ownership of my gut and to feel good. Today, this way of eating has become so ingrained in me that if I am feeling bloated, I know to stay away from onions and larger amounts of bread.

Throughout this book, I am going to empower you with information so you can take charge, too—and move on with your life and your healthy gut. I will talk to you one-on-one just as I would talk to one of my patients. I want you to feel comfortable because I am asking you to make some big changes to your diet.

What Are FODMAPs?

a.k.a. the science of how these weird sounding categories of foods are digested—or not digested

The low-FODMAP diet can be very confusing because there are a lot of particulars that you have to remember. In chapter 3, I am going to guide you through an elimination diet to test whether FODMAPs may be the culprits for your digestive distress. But first, I am taking the liberty of simplifying things for you. Even though I am going to go through all of the science—so you will know that this is legit!—when it comes to making lists and asking you to remember things, I am going to keep it as simple as possible.

FODMAP stands for: **f**ermentable **o**ligosaccharides, **d**isaccharides, **m**onosaccharides, **and** **p**olyols. These are foods that are high in the carbohydrates lactose, fructose, galacto-oligosaccharides (GOS), fructans, sorbitol, and mannitol. If you suspect sensitivity to FODMAPs, you may have a sensitivity to one, some, or all of these categories.

All of the foods in the photograph on the left are healthy, but which of them are high in FODMAPs? By the end of this book, you'll be able to identify them for yourself.

FODMAP

CAN YOU SPELL IT OUT FOR ME?

The **F** is for *fermentable*, foods that can make you bloated. This is an umbrella term that encompasses the other FODMAPs. Fermentable foods are carbohydrates that are easily broken down by bacteria in your gut. When the bacteria chow down on them, they produce hydrogen, carbon dioxide, and methane gases that can leave you feeling bloated.

> **Fermentable vs. Fermented**
> Fermentable foods are not the same as fermented foods. Fermented foods, such as miso and kombucha, have already been broken down by bacteria.

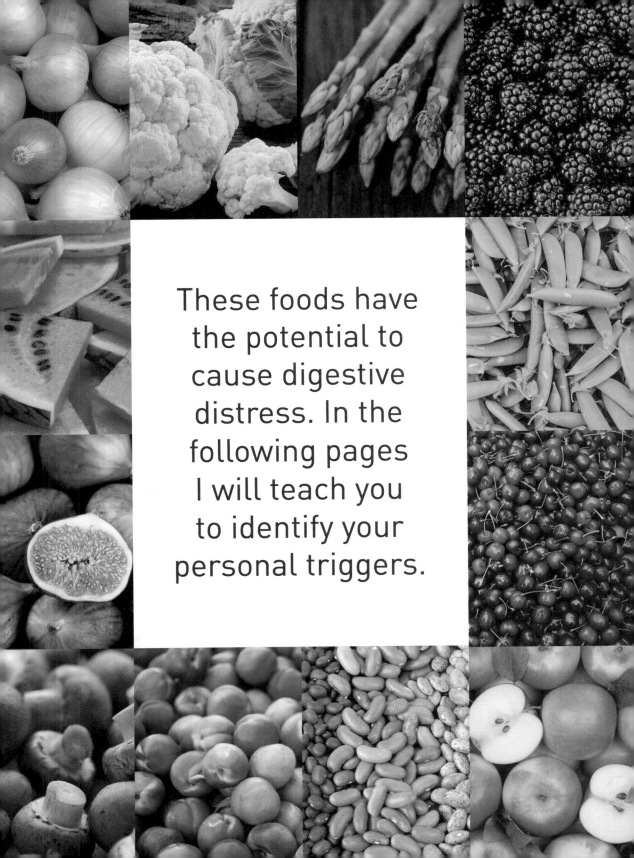

These foods have the potential to cause digestive distress. In the following pages I will teach you to identify your personal triggers.

FODMAP

The **O** is for *oligosaccharides*, a fancy word for a short chain of carbohydrates. This is a diverse group of foods that have one big thing in common: they are difficult to digest, so they can cause digestive distress. There are two categories of foods that fall under oligosaccharides: fructans and galacto-oligosaccharides (GOS). Fructans are a carbohydrate found in a variety of foods including wheat, onions, and garlic, among others. Galacto-oligosaccharides are a carbohydrate found primarily in beans.

Fructans

Although wheat is high in fructans, fructans are not related to gluten (which is a protein); they just coincide in many of the same foods. *Fructose* and *fructans* are also similar words—but they are components of different foods. Fructose is most commonly found in fruits. Fructans are prevalent in wheat, garlic, onions, and other vegetables.

OLIGOSACCHARIDES: GOS AND FRUCTANS

High
Barley
Beans
Chamomile tea
Cashews
Dates
Dried figs
Fennel tea
Leeks
Onions
Shallots
Soybeans
Garlic
Inulin (a.k.a. chicory root/FOS)
Nectarines
Oolong tea
Pistachios
Plums
Prunes
Rye
Watermelon
Wheat
White peaches

Low
Less than ¼ cup of canned
  chickpeas
Less than ½ cup of canned
  lentils
The green part of the leeks
  and scallions
Garlic-infused oil

FODMAP

The **D** is for *disaccharides*, literally "two sugars," which in this case refers to lactose. Lactose is a sugar naturally found in milk. It is made up of two other sugars, glucose and galactose, that are linked together. Humans can't digest these two together without the help of an enzyme called lactase. A significant portion of the population lacks this enzyme. If you do not have a sufficient quantity of lactase enzyme, then you are lactose intolerant.

Not all dairy products contain lactose. Check out these lists to see which dairy products contain lactose.

DISACCHARIDES: LACTOSE

High	Low
Cottage cheese	Butter
Cream cheese	Cheddar
Ice cream	Feta
Milk	Lactose-free milk
Ricotta	Lactose-free yogurt
Yogurt	Parmesan
	Swiss

FODMAP

The **M** is for *monosaccharides*, meaning "one sugar." Fructose is a monosaccharide, and fructose is a FODMAP! Fructose is a sugar naturally found in fruits. While all fruits contain sugar, it only becomes problematic in those people who are sensitive to it when the amount of fructose in a food is greater than the amount of glucose. How do you know which fruits have more fructose than glucose? Check out my lists.

MONOSACCHARIDES: FRUCTOSE

High	Low
Agave nectar	Bananas
Apples	Blueberries
Asparagus	Coconut
Cherries	Lemons
High-fructose corn syrup	Limes
Fresh figs	Oranges
Honey	Pineapple
Jerusalem artichokes (a.k.a. sunchokes)	Raspberries
	Strawberries
Mangoes	
Pears	
Sugar snap peas	
Watermelon	

FODMAP

The **A** is for *and*. The **P** is for *polyols*. Polyols are sugar alcohols that appear in the diet naturally in certain fruits and vegetables; they are also used as artificial sweeteners. Polyols naturally occur in stone fruits, such as prunes (which is why prunes help with constipation), snow peas, and mushrooms. There are two categories of polyols that naturally occur in foods: sorbitol and mannitol, carbohydrates that are very similar in structure but are prevalent in different foods.

Artificial Sweeteners

Sorbitol, mannitol, maltitol, isolmalt, and xylitol are high-FODMAP ingredients that are commonly used as artificial sweeteners. You will find these in beverages and foods that are advertised as "sugar-free," such as sodas and gum, because they are a way to sweeten without adding calories. My trick? Don't use sweeteners that end in *-ol*!

POLYOLS: SORBITOL AND MANNITOL

High
Apples
Apricots
Blackberries
Cauliflower
Mushrooms
Nectarines
Peaches
Pears
Plums
Prunes
Snow peas
Sweet corn
Watermelon

Low
Blueberries
Dried cranberries (small
  amounts)
Green beans
Strawberries
Stevia
Table sugar

PORTION SIZES MATTER

It isn't *totally* accurate to say that this diet can be simplified into yes–and–no food lists, though those lists are a very important and critical part of the diet. The other essential big-picture thinking is that *portion sizes matter*. This is because some foods that are generally considered low-FODMAP can aggravate sensitivities when consumed in higher quantities. You will notice that I list portion sizes for certain foods and not for others. When I list specific portion sizes, it means that the food has been tested in a laboratory and been found to be high-FODMAP when consumed in more than the stated quantity.

⅛ Avocado—Are You Kidding?

Sometimes when I say something like that only ⅛ avocado is okay for the elimination phase, it can drive people a little crazy because it is such a small and specific amount. But sometimes I am going to limit portions on certain foods—only because that is what the research says. Try to think of it this way—you can have sushi that has a little avocado in it and not worry about it. For now, though, hold off on heaping avocado on your toast. You can compromise by having a slice of suitable gluten-free bread with ⅛ avocado smeared on it, and a fried egg on top. Luckily, I can tell you from my experience that most of my patients are able to tolerate more than ⅛ avocado after the elimination phase.

FODMAPS HAVE ADDITIVE EFFECTS

The reason I am putting you on an elimination diet is that it is hard to figure out what foods cause reactions. Sometimes you might think that you are lactose intolerant, but other times you can have yogurt and feel fine. Why would that be the case? Because FODMAPs have cumulative effects.

You might be fine with some yogurt if you are not eating other high-FODMAP foods. But if you had yogurt with honey in the morning, an apple as a snack, and an asparagus salad for lunch—you may find yourself bloated and uncomfortable. It is possible that each of these high-FODMAP choices on its own is not enough to cause trouble—but when you have multiple high-FODMAP foods together, they cause you to reach a threshold where the symptoms start.

You may be able to handle small amounts of FODMAPs, but having too many FODMAP foods can have a cumulative effect.

Is Low-FODMAP Right for You?

(2)

IBS

Are you one of the 10 to 20 percent of Americans who suffer from irritable bowel syndrome (IBS)? It is pretty shocking to think that up to one in five people in the United States are affected by IBS. It's something a lot of people don't really like talking about—which makes sense because it can be painful, uncomfortable, and embarrassing. IBS is a symptom-based condition: There is no widely accepted diagnostic test for it at this time, which means that diagnosing IBS relies on symptoms that a patient reports to the doctor—in this case, someone who complains of abdominal pain *and* constipation or diarrhea. IBS is incredibly common, and yet many suffer in silence.

The international standard definition of IBS is determined by the Rome Foundation, an independent not-for-profit organization made up of a group of over 80 scientists from around the world who collaborate to write the classification for IBS and other functional gut disorders. A functional gut disorder is a condition that affects function but cannot be seen (that is to say, tests and scans do not pick up abnormalities). Despite not being visible, functional gut disorders are burdensome, while carrying the extra load of having a difficult diagnostic process. The Rome Criteria is an attempt to quantify the constellation of symptoms surrounding IBS. The most recent definition is presented in the Rome IV Criteria published in 2016. It defines IBS as abdominal pain accompanied by at least two of the following three symptoms: pain associated with going to the bathroom, change in frequency of bowel movements, and change in form of bowel movements (that is, constipation or diarrhea) at least once a week over the last three months.

There are a variety of treatment offerings for IBS, but a number of forward-thinking doctors have come to realize that diet should be front and center when treating this syndrome; indeed, some now believe that it should be the first line of treatment. If you are suffering from the symptoms of IBS—such as constipation, diarrhea, pain, gas, or bloating—the good news is that the low-FODMAP diet has been shown in a major study conducted in Australia to help up to 75 percent of IBS sufferers. As far as scientific studies go, that is a very promising statistic.

The first-of-its-kind randomized controlled FODMAP research study in the United States was conducted with IBS patients by doctors at the University of Michigan—and the research is so new, at the time of writing the studies have not even been published. The results were, however, presented in San Diego in 2016 at the largest national digestive health conference, Digestive Disease Week. Ninety IBS patients were prescribed a diet—half low-FODMAP, half a "common sense" diet consisting of such suggestions as eating smaller meals and avoiding caffeine and alcohol. To summarize the results, *50 percent* of the patients treated with the low-FODMAP diet enjoyed significant relief of IBS symptoms, compared to 20 percent in the control group. The symptoms most likely to improve were abdominal pain and bloating, and more than half of the people on the low-FODMAP diet reported improved quality of life. These are very encouraging results.

SIBO

Emerging research suggests that the underlying cause of the symptoms in many cases of IBS is a condition called small intestinal bacterial overgrowth (SIBO). SIBO diagnosis has become incredibly common in my practice.

What Is SIBO?

SIBO is a condition in which there is too much bacteria in the small intestine. Even though the bacteria might be beneficial in nature, and are not necessarily pathogenic (bad), you can have too much of a good thing and you can have it in the wrong places.

In the normal digestive process, most of our food is broken down in the stomach and then absorbed in the small intestine. The food that is not digestible (fiber) makes it to the large intestine, where bacteria help break it down. We want to have a lot of bacteria in our *large* intestine. There is substantial research showing that bacteria in our large intestine helps digest fibers, produce vitamins, and block out bad bacteria that will make us sick.

While we want to have a lot of bacteria in our large intestine, we should have relatively few in our *small* intestine. If you have a lot of bacteria in your small intestine, it will start eating food that is slow to get digested (because it is just sitting there waiting to be digested). High-FODMAP foods are digested poorly and slowly, making them the perfect feast for hungry bacteria. The bacteria find these foods, eat them, and then produce their own by-product (gas)—causing your bloated abdomen and other digestive symptoms.

Because bacteria love FODMAPs, and SIBO is an overgrowth of bacteria, reducing the amount of FODMAPs you consume will keep down the amount of bacteria present in your small intestine.

There are many factors that can cause SIBO. They include, but are not limited to: celiac disease; inflammatory bowel diseases such as Crohn's disease and ulcerative colitis; diabetes; prior abdominal surgery; food poisoning; and multiple rounds of antibiotics. Pinpointing the cause of SIBO is helpful to prevent recurrence, because without knowing the mechanism, it is not possible to treat the root cause.

How to Diagnose SIBO

SIBO is still a relatively new diagnosis, and the availability of testing can be limited. The best way to test for SIBO is using a breath test that measures the amount of hydrogen and methane gases produced by the bacteria in your digestive system over a three-hour period. This can be done in a doctor's office or with a kit that your doctor prescribes, which you take home and then mail to a laboratory.

Before you take the breath test, you will have a limited diet for 24 hours. Samples of your breath will be taken by blowing into a tube: First, you will take a baseline measure of your breath. Then, you will imbibe a solution of either lactulose or glucose (depending on what your practitioner decides), and continue to provide breath samples every 20 to 30 minutes for three hours.

The results are analyzed for the presence of hydrogen and methane gases, both of which are produced by bacteria. Your doctor can chart the amount of these gases in your breath over a period of time, an analog for how much bacteria is at different points in your digestive tract. (We know typical transit times through your digestive system, which gives us an idea of where the solute is at a given point in time.)

Different types of bacteria will produce hydrogen and methane, so seeing the levels of both of these gases gives more information as to the type of bacteria that is present. It can help your doctor make a decision about the type of antibiotic to give you as treatment (more on that in a moment). Bacteria that produce methane can be more difficult to eradicate. Methane-producing bacteria tend to cause more constipation and bloating, whereas hydrogen-producing bacteria tend to cause more loose stool.

Lactose and Fructose Breath Tests

You can also take a breath test to diagnose lactose intolerance and fructose malabsorption. The process will be exactly the same as described for SIBO breath testing, but the substrate will be either lactose or fructose. You can take a lactose breath test as an alternative to self-testing (which I describe in chapter 4). You can also take a fructose breath test—but it tends to yield false positives: the result may be positive whether or not consuming fructose causes symptoms. For this reason, I believe that testing fructose by using food and assessing your reaction, also discussed in chapter 4, is a more effective diagnostic tool.

Reducing the amount of FODMAPs you consume will keep down the amount of bacteria present in your small intestine.

Treating SIBO

Research is still actively under way for the best course of treatment for this condition. The doctors that I work with tend to prescribe a course of antibiotics followed by a low-FODMAP diet. It may sound surprising to use antibiotics, since we know that bacteria can be good for you. With SIBO, the bacteria might be good, but there is still too much of them, and in the wrong place, and the way to reduce this is through using antibiotics. Some practitioners will also prescribe herbal antimicrobials that can achieve the same goal. Recommendations for treatment continue to evolve, as this is an emerging field. Anecdotally I see the combination of antibiotics followed by the low-FODMAP diet working for my patients as a way to keep SIBO from recurring as well as for symptom management.

SIBO

Samantha, age 20, was a college student who came in to see me with her mother when she was home from school. She had actually at that point taken a break from school because her digestive symptoms—bloating and diarrhea—had taken over her life. She was not able to sit through a lecture without needing to go to the bathroom. She was also a dancer, and her symptoms were interfering in a major way. Samantha had had her appendix removed two years prior—and though she was told that everything would go back to normal after the procedure, this was not what she experienced. Ever since the surgery, she had been plagued by these issues.

She had been to numerous doctors, and none of them asked her what she ate. Given her history of abdominal surgery and that the symptoms started after the surgery, I suspected SIBO. Luckily, when Samantha came to see me, I was able to talk to her doctor and ask for a lactulose breath test. The test results confirmed the diagnosis of SIBO. I met with Samantha during her course of antibiotics, to instruct her on the low-FODMAP diet that she would begin as soon as she finished the medication. She started to feel a bit better after the antibiotics—but when she started the low-FODMAP diet, she felt dramatically better within two days. This is not an exaggeration. We met again two days later to come up with a game plan.

She looked at the list of high-FODMAP foods that I gave her—and she noticed immediately that it included a few foods she was eating on a very regular basis. If you are experiencing symptoms *frequently*, foods that are consumed *infrequently* are likely not the cause. In Samantha's case, bread, mangoes, and yogurt jumped out at her as foods that she ate all the time. For her, the elimination diet meant swapping out her bread for a suitable gluten-free option, eating one portion of low-FODMAP fruit at a time, and switching to lactose-free yogurt. She liked having eggs in the morning, a peanut butter sandwich for lunch, and chicken with grilled vegetables for dinner. With these minor swaps, she was able to enjoy a wide variety of foods.

Samantha continued to limit lactose, fructose, and fructans in her diet for the long term, but was perfectly happy doing so. She did not think of it as a sacrifice at all. Her success on the low-FODMAP diet was dramatic, and she was thrilled to return to college the next semester feeling great. She was able to resume dancing with her team—which she had not thought possible after two years of suffering.

CELIAC DISEASE

When one has an autoimmune disease, the body starts attacking itself. In celiac disease, the body attacks the small intestine—and it only does so in the presence of gluten. When your small intestine is attacked, its villi, fingerlike projections that absorb nutrients, get damaged. Without villi it becomes difficult to absorb the nutrients you need from your food. The only known treatment for celiac disease is strict adherence to a gluten-free diet.

Unfortunately, the Celiac Disease Foundation estimates that up to 20 percent of people with celiac disease continue to have symptoms while on a gluten-free diet. I have seen several patients over the years who have celiac disease whose symptoms do not subside on the gluten-free diet alone. This is obviously very frustrating for these patients because they are making a great effort to stay 100 percent gluten-free and yet still feel no relief. The low-FODMAP diet is one potential way to provide relief in patients who are not helped by the gluten-free diet alone. These patients still need to be 100 percent gluten-free and avoid cross-contamination. But removing high-FODMAP foods can help them feel better.

Screening for Celiac Disease

If you have been experiencing gastrointestinal (GI) symptoms, you may also want to ask your doctor about testing for celiac disease. It is important to find out whether you have celiac disease *before* cutting gluten out of your diet, because you will need to have gluten in your system to be tested properly for this disease. Even though you may feel better by not eating gluten, you will want to have accurate testing, because if you do have celiac disease, there are other things your doctor will want to monitor. A doctor can test you for celiac disease by using a blood test and/or biopsy. Typically, the first step is to analyze your blood for the tissue transglutaminase (tTG) antibody, which indicates levels of intestinal inflammation. Then, if needed, your doctor may follow up with a small bowel biopsy to examine the villi of your small intestine. Since the villi get damaged in celiac disease, a biopsy would allow your doctor to visualize the condition of the villi.

Gluten and FODMAPs

As the gluten-free diet is a popular diet trend and there is some overlap between it and the low-FODMAP diet, is it easier to think of this diet as gluten-free? When it comes to explaining this to your friends—yes. But actually, from a scientific standpoint, gluten and FODMAPs are totally different. *Gluten is a protein, whereas FODMAPs are carbohydrates.* What do they have in common? Both are found in wheat, barley, and rye. Confused? Foods are complex. Wheat is made of many components—some carbohydrates, some protein, even some fat. While the carbohydrate portion of wheat houses FODMAPs, the protein portion houses gluten. Therefore, when you take whole wheat and grind it up, the resulting flour will be high in FODMAPs as well as in gluten.

Gluten-Free Bread May Not Be Low-FODMAP Bread
Although we established that wheat is high in both gluten and FODMAPs, not all gluten-free bread is low-FODMAP. Even without wheat, gluten-free bread can be filled with all sorts of other ingredients, specifically sweeteners—I have seen gluten-free breads made with high-fructose corn syrup, apple or pear puree, inulin, honey, and agave nectar. While these breads are gluten-free, they are not low-FODMAP.

Also, some foods that contain gluten, such as soy sauce and seitan, are low-FODMAP.

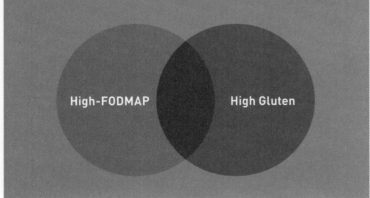

High-FODMAP   High Gluten

CELIAC DISEASE

Sarah, age 32, came into my office feeling distraught. She had been diagnosed with celiac disease after years of doctor's visits—with complaints of significant digestive discomfort, including bloating and diarrhea. She was actually relieved to get the diagnosis, as surprising as that sounds. She felt that now that she had this diagnosis, there was a straightforward prescription for what to do. The only treatment for celiac disease is to consume a 100 percent gluten-free diet. So, that is what she did—and she committed herself to it completely. You can imagine how upset she was a year later when she came to see me, feeling no better than she did before starting the gluten-free diet. How could this be? She had tried so hard!

Sarah and I went over a three-day diet record, as I do with all of my patients. I like to have a sense of what they are eating on two weekdays and one weekend day, so I can see how the days differ, and also what foods recur on a more regular basis. I learn what types of food each individual prefers—and it gives me a chance to tailor a diet plan to make it realistic for them to follow. Looking at a diet record gives me a sense of whether the patients are eating meals or grazing throughout the day. I also have them include the times during the day when they are experiencing symptoms, so I can start to get a picture of the relationship between what they are eating and how it may be making them feel.

In Sarah's case, looking at her diet record showed that she was doing a diligent job of following a gluten-free diet. This is not always the case; I have seen many patients who have celiac disease but have not been careful about avoiding cross-contamination sources of gluten. I always want to rule out gluten cross-contamination before introducing a new diet.

Unfortunately, Sarah's is a common story. She was diagnosed (using a hydrogen breath test) with SIBO in addition to celiac disease—and in her case, the low-FODMAP diet in addition to the gluten-free diet was just what she needed to finally get rid of her symptoms. Looking at her diet record, I found that she would have gluten-free bread, peanut butter, and bananas for breakfast. On first glance this might seem totally benign. However, when I did some deeper digging, I found that the delicious gluten-free bread that she was buying from this new bakery used apple puree as a main ingredient. Since apples are high in fructose and sorbitol, I identified this bread as one of the foods that was causing trouble. Switching the type of gluten-free bread that Sarah was eating was one easy place to start. She was prone to skipping lunch and snacking on an apple and popcorn in the afternoon. I suggested switching the apple for an orange, which has easier-to-digest sugars. For dinner she might have gluten-free pasta with pesto. Instead, I suggested swapping out the pesto in favor of garlic-infused oil and Parmesan. Although the garlic in her pesto is high-FODMAP, garlic-infused oil is surprisingly not! Sarah loved pesto and did end up making my low-FODMAP version; however, it was more manageable for her to start off this dietary experiment without undertaking much cooking.

Sarah had already become accustomed to making big changes to her diet since her celiac disease diagnosis. Yet asking her to cut out additional foods—even as a test—made her feel stressed. To make it work for her, we worked closely together to make sure she didn't feel deprived. I thought that if I could accommodate some of her less healthy preferences, she would be more likely to feel better in the long term. To appease her sweet tooth, I even gave her low-FODMAP candy options, because that was the one thing that made her

feel good *emotionally* as she started the elimination diet.

Sarah ended up feeling better when she was on the low-FODMAP diet, particularly when she was avoiding foods in the fructan category—namely onions and garlic. However, in the long term she decided not to be too strict about it. She was resentful about having to make additional specifications (on top of being gluten-free) when she was eating out, so she would occasionally decide to suffer the consequences of eating foods that she knew would bother her. In Sarah's case, if she "cheated" and ended up with diarrhea, she would take an over-the-counter remedy that eased some of her discomfort. Even when she didn't stick to the strictest version of her plan, she felt empowered in knowing exactly what she could eat to feel her best.

NONCELIAC GLUTEN SENSITIVITY

Some individuals experience similar symptoms to the ones caused by celiac disease—including digestive complaints—but do not have positive tTG blood test results and do not have damage to the small intestine. Nonetheless, these individuals claim to feel better when removing gluten from their diet. This is a field of active research. There is evidence to suggest that it may be FODMAPs causing trouble for these individuals, not gluten.

People who do not have celiac disease and who believe they are gluten intolerant may actually be symptomatic due to the FODMAPs, not the gluten!

If you do not have celiac disease, even if you are sensitive to fructans (the FODMAP found in wheat), you will likely be able to tolerate small portions of wheat—such as bread crumbs. Cross-contamination of gluten is not an issue with the low-FODMAP diet because the portion size of wheat that would be inadvertently ingested is not enough to set off symptoms.

TAKING INVENTORY

It is helpful to take inventory of your symptoms before you embark on the low-FODMAP, a.k.a. "healthy gut," diet. Trust me, if you don't document how you feel before you start, you will forget how bad it was as soon as you feel better. It is so easy to forget feeling lousy. I certainly don't want you to dwell on feeling bad, but I do think it is helpful to remember exactly how things were when you started the diet, so you can evaluate whether anything has changed. Then, you can look back and say, "My belly pain went from once a day to once a month," for example. If you don't keep track by using a simple methodology, such as the chart in the back of this book, then you might experience the same improvement but think to yourself, "I had stomachaches, but now I still have them," without taking into consideration how infrequently they occur. Since this diet is based on science, let's make ourselves data scientists—it will just take a minute. Turn to page 172 and complete the "Frequency Before Low-FODMAP Diet" column of the symptom chart.

How frequently are you experiencing symptoms?

AM I GOING TO LOSE WEIGHT ON THIS DIET?

This book is designed using the latest science to help you reduce the bloat that you are carrying around your waist. The low-FODMAP diet is a tool to pinpoint the culprits so you can live the life you want. In and of itself, it is not necessarily a weight-loss diet, but this book will provide healthy recipes and strategies to maintain or lose weight on a low-FODMAP diet.

The Elimination Diet—You Can Do It

How am I really going to do this? In other words: calm me down, please

You can do it. Trust me, I've walked hundreds of people through this diet. Once you learn how to follow the plan, you won't even need *all* new recipes—make some slight modifications to the way you were eating before and you are all set. It might mean switching out a vegetable side at dinner, changing up the milk you have with your oatmeal, swapping out an ingredient in a smoothie— but you can and will find the culprits that cause digestive distress and then replace them without causing a major frenzy.

This is not an all-or-nothing diet. If you "cheat" or "screw up," it's okay; just get back on track as soon as possible. If you do stray from the low-FODMAP path, you might feel some of the symptoms you started with (that is the worst-case scenario), but it will not derail your progress. Lapses happen. It might take a day or two to feel better, but try not to stress too much about it. It won't cause a long-term setback. Plus, once you are feeling your best, you will feel so great that won't even want to cheat.

Go with your gut (instincts): If you look at the lists of high-FODMAP foods that I provide on pages 49–50 and see certain foods that you eat a lot of, cut back on those and see how you feel. Yes, going on an elimination diet is a commitment, and this might seem like a pain, but the truth is that if you are feeling better, you might not really care about taking this stuff out—it may not feel like a compromise if you stop experiencing your gastrointestinal complaints. Plus, you might not even be eating a lot of high-FODMAP foods to begin with—so, you may not be eliminating that many things.

This is not an all-or-nothing diet. If you "cheat" or "screw up," it's okay; just get back on track as soon as possible.

HOW DOES THE ELIMINATION DIET WORK?

An elimination diet is when you identify all the foods that could potentially be causing you trouble and remove them from your diet *entirely and all at once*. Then you assess how you feel without the potential culprits. Once you feel better, it is time to test the foods you have taken out of your diet, in a systematic, gradual way, so that you can figure out which ones caused your symptoms. I will also explain a "Simple Option" that allows you to test your tolerance of one category of FODMAPs at a time.

THE ELIMINATION DIET PLAN

Phase 1: elimination
Phase 2: testing
Phase 3: personalization

GUIDE THROUGH THE ELIMINATION DIET

Preparation

You can do certain things to get yourself ready to start this diet. This will require some planning and grocery shopping.

Embarking on this diet plan does not mean that you need to walk around your kitchen with a giant garbage bag, throwing everything out that is on the "no" list, because the "no" list is really "no just for the time being." You may find that foods on the "no" list end up being perfectly fine for you after the elimination phase is over. But I will not dissuade you from throwing out junk food and anything that is expired!

Plan meals ahead of time, especially if you know that you are going to be eating out. You might want to look online or call to get the menu ahead of time, so you will know what you can order. (For helpful tips, see my guide to eating out on pages 97–99.)

Stock your kitchen. Load up on the ingredients that you will need to succeed during the elimination phase—many of these

items are things that you already have or are available at your local grocery store. It can be motivating and empowering to go grocery shopping and have fresh new produce to enjoy during the elimination phase. Even though you are removing foods from your diet, it does not mean that you can't enjoy the ones that you are allowed to eat.

Put your food on display. It will create a psychological shift if see cut-up carrots and peppers when you open your refrigerator or have a bowl of fresh bananas and oranges out on your counter. You will see that you have something to grab in a pinch and can feel good about eating.

WHAT IF A FOOD I LIKE IS NOT ON ANY OF YOUR LISTS?

I get questions from people all of the time about whether some obscure food is low-FODMAP or not. I am reliant (as is everyone in this field) on laboratory research to test new foods. I can use my judgment and knowledge of foods that have been tested to give my best guess on foods that are combinations of things (that is, made up of many ingredients that have individually been tested). However, if one of the ingredients has unknown FODMAP content, I will not be able to tell you whether it will work for you. My solution to this problem is to tell people to avoid any unknown FODMAP foods during the elimination phase. Then, when you are doing the testing to figure out your tolerance for the different FODMAP categories, if there is a food that you miss terribly, and we don't know where it fits in, add that food to your list for testing and see how it works for you.

The Elimination Phase

You will want to stay on the elimination diet for at least two weeks. If you start to feel better right away, that is a great sign and it means that a change that you made is helping you. You can stay on the elimination diet for several weeks, but the goal is not to stay on it *unnecessarily* for the long term. The plan is to cut out high-FODMAP foods for the elimination phase and then go through and test certain high-FODMAP foods, one at a time, to

How You Eat

In addition to changing up your diet, you can improve digestion by being more aware of how you eat. Keep these suggestions in mind both during and after the "diet" phase of the plan:

Take your time. We are all busy and have gotten accustomed to eating breakfast in our car or lunch at our desk. Taking your time with a meal will give you a chance to chew your food well, and chewing is the first step for healthy digestion because it starts breaking the food down.

Eat mindfully. Being distracted often means not paying attention to what your body is telling you. Should you slow down? Are you full? You need to be focused to tell.

Eat five small meals a day. Sometimes part of the problem with a big or bloated abdomen is just about the quantity of food. You could be making good choices but perhaps you only have one or two meals a day and you are hungry, so the meals are very large. Eating five smaller meals spread throughout the day can help let your body digest the smaller quantities of food.

Sit upright. Ideally, we should all be waiting two hours after a meal before lying down. It can help prevent heartburn and acid reflux symptoms.

Take a walk. If you are looking to avoid lying down after a meal, the perfect thing to do is to take a walk. Even just a short walk around the block can help get your digestion moving.

Stay hydrated. The importance of hydration can't be overstated here. One of the most common issues I see with patients is poor hydration. Buy a 32-ounce water bottle and aim to refill it once during the day (64 ounces total).

But not from a straw. Drinking from a straw introduces extra air into your system, not unlike chewing gum. It could cause gas, burping, or bloating. This may or may not bother you—but if it strikes a chord, you might want to try cutting back on using straws.

determine which culprits were causing your symptoms. You may think of the elimination phase as a low-FODMAP tool to assess your tolerance to certain foods.

STARTING THE ELIMINATION DIET

It's the moment you've been waiting for: You are ready to begin the elimination diet. Get ready to eliminate your bloated belly.

You are going to be eating only foods on the following "yes" list and avoiding foods on the "no" list. This book is chock-full of meal ideas to get you inspired as well as tweaks to help you make small changes to what you would normally be eating. Remember that portion sizes matter, and that even though here I am breaking it down into simple lists of "yes" and "no," that "yes" does not mean unlimited quantity. Refer to pages 175–77 for specific information on portions.

It can take a little while to get the hang of things when you are making a significant change to your diet—especially one like this where you are eliminating a whole array of foods that don't seem to be so closely related to one another. By week two, it should start to become second nature. You don't need to write down everything that you are eating, but week two is a good time to check in with yourself: What issues are you having? Where do you need help? Do you need extra support on this journey?

After two weeks, if you feel that you still need a little more time to get yourself together, extend the elimination phase for a week or more, as needed, before proceeding to the testing phase.

You may particularly want to stay on the elimination diet for more time if you suffer from constipation. Constipation is the symptom that tends to take the longest to respond to dietary changes—which makes sense if you think about constipation as general digestive slowness.

When you are ready, or by the time you have been on the elimination diet for three weeks, it is time to take inventory of your symptoms again. You can record them in the "elimination phase" column of the chart on page 172.

SO, WHAT CAN YOU EAT?—FOODS FOR THE ELIMINATION DIET

By now you're probably wondering what all the fuss is about—what are these high- and low-FODMAP foods and what can you eat during the elimination phase? I am presenting the lists of food to incorporate and to exclude in two formats. One list is by FODMAP category and the other is by grocery category (grouped by fruits, vegetables, etc.). I find that my patients enjoy having both lists available. You will find the full list of foods to include during the elimination phase—and appropriate portion sizes—on pages 58–59.

Following these lists of foods is a sample seven-day meal plan (and a shopping list for everything you'll need for it) to show you how easy—and delicious—it can be to stick to the elimination diet. You will find each of these recipes in chapter 7, and pages 178–80 provide a handy list of brand-name foods that are low in FODMAPs and easy to find.

FOODS TO AVOID DURING THE ELIMINATION PHASE BY FODMAP CATEGORY

LACTOSE

Dairy: cottage cheese, cream, ice cream, milk, ricotta, yogurt

FRUCTOSE

Sweeteners: agave nectar, high-fructose corn syrup, honey
Fruits: apples, cherries (more than 3), figs, mangoes, pears, watermelon
Vegetables: asparagus, fava beans, Jerusalem artichokes (a.k.a. sunchokes), sugar snap peas

FRUCTANS

Fruits: dates, dried apricots, dried figs, dried mangoes, dried pineapple, goji berries (more than 1 tablespoon), nectarines, prunes, raisins, snow peas, watermelon, white peaches
Vegetables: artichokes, beets (more than 2 slices), cabbage (more than ½ cup), garlic, leeks, onions

Grains: barley, rye, wheat

Nuts: cashews, pistachios

GOS

Beans: black beans, chickpeas, lima beans, navy beans, red kidney beans, soybeans

SORBITOL

Fruits: apples, apricots, avocados, blackberries, nectarines, pears, peaches, plums, prunes

Vegetables: broccoli (large quantities), sweet corn

MANNITOL

Vegetables: cauliflower, mushrooms, snow peas

Fruit: watermelon

POLYOLS

Artificial sweeteners: sorbitol, mannitol, maltitol, xylitol

SO WHAT CAN YOU DRINK?—BEVERAGES FOR THE ELIMINATION DIET

What you drink is very important as you could certainly overload on FODMAPs from beverages alone. Let's get the things you have to avoid out of the way so that we can focus on some fun drink ideas that are low-FODMAP. I have included beverage recipes in chapter 7.

> **High-FODMAP drinks/drink ingredients to avoid:**
> Agave nectar, apple juice, chamomile tea, fennel tea, honey, high-fructose corn syrup, mango juice/puree, oolong tea, more than ½ cup of orange juice, pear juice, rum, sorbitol (artificial sweetener), watermelon juice.
> I will admit that it comes as quite a surprise to me that chamomile tea registers in the laboratory as a high-FODMAP food, considering one often thinks of chamomile as soothing.

Other considerations for beverages on the low-FODMAP diet: although carbonation is not a FODMAP, it may still bother you. Also, beer and other liquors are low FODMAP, yet they are certainly potential culprits for digestive distress—I do not recommend drinking beer, and I suggest limiting alcohol consumption in general. That doesn't mean you can't enjoy a nice glass of wine, or one cocktail with suitable ingredients.

I've mentioned it before, but it really cannot be overstated that it is important to maintain proper hydration by drinking water.

Here are some drink ideas to try if you get bored with water:

- Hot or iced green tea with a wedge of lemon
- Golden Milk (page 106)
- Hot or iced Chai Latte (page 105) made with almond milk
- Hot water with wedge of lemon
- Juice made of low-FODMAP vegetables and fruits (page 107)
- Smoothie made from low-FODMAP vegetables and fruits (page 109)
- Hot or iced coffee with almond milk
- Sparkling water (if tolerated) with dash of orange or cranberry juice
- Flavored sparkling water (if tolerated)
- Water mixed with True Citrus brand crystallized citrus juice (lemon, lime, or orange)

These drinks are also suitable for the elimination diet:

- Black, white, or peppermint tea (1 cup)
- Coffee (1 cup)
- Cocoa made from 2 tablespoons cocoa powder and almond milk or lactose-free milk
- Coconut water (less than ½ cup)
- Cranberry juice (1 cup)
- Orange juice (up to ½ cup)
- Tomato juice (1 cup)

LOW-FODMAP AND HIGH-FODMAP FOODS BY GROCERY CATEGORY

During the elimination phase, the foods marked with an asterisk in this chart should be eaten in limited quantities, as described in the portion sizes that follow and on pages 175–77.

	YES = LOW FODMAP	NO = HIGH FODMAP
Fruits	Avocados*, bananas, blueberries, cantaloupe, clementines, coconut*, dragon fruit, dried bananas, dried cranberries*, grapes, guavas, honeydew melon, kiwis, kumquats, lemons, limes, oranges, papaya, passion fruit, pineapple, plantains, pomegranates*, prickly pears, raspberries, rhubarb, star fruit, strawberries	Apples, apricots, blackberries, cherries, dates, fresh/dried figs, grapefruit, mangoes, nectarines, peaches, pears, plums, prunes, watermelon, white peaches
Vegetables	Alfalfa sprouts, bean sprouts, beets*, bell peppers (any color), bok choy, broccoli*, Brussels sprouts*, butternut squash*, cabbage*, carrots, celeriac, celery, cherry tomatoes, chile peppers, chives, collard greens, corn*, cucumber, eggplant, endive, fennel, fresh tomatoes, galangal, ginger, green beans, kabocha squash, kale, leek leaves (green part only), lettuce, okra, olives, parsnips, pumpkin (canned), radishes, scallions (green part only), seaweed, snow peas*, spaghetti squash, spinach, summer squash, sun-dried tomatoes*, sweet potatoes*, Swiss chard, taro, tomatoes (canned), turnips, water chestnuts, white potatoes, zucchini	Asparagus, cauliflower, garlic, Jerusalem artichokes (a.k.a. sunchokes), leeks, mushrooms, onions, peas, shallots, sugar snap peas
Dairy	Almond milk, canned coconut milk, Cheddar, feta, goat cheese, lactose-free cottage cheese, lactose-free milk, lactose-free yogurt, Parmesan, rice milk, Swiss	Cottage cheese, cream cheese, ice cream, milk, ricotta, yogurt
Grains	Almond flour, amaranth, brown rice, oat bran, oats, polenta, popcorn, quinoa, suitable gluten-free breads and pastas, white rice	Barley, rye, wheat

	✓	✗
Nuts and seeds	Almonds*, chia seeds, flaxseeds, hazelnuts, hemp seeds, pecans, pumpkin seeds, sunflower seeds, walnuts	Cashews, pistachios
Proteins	Beef, chickpeas (canned)*, chicken, eggs, firm tofu, fish, lamb, canned lentils (canned)*, mollusks (clams, mussels, oysters), pork, salmon, sardines, scallops, shellfish (lobster, shrimp), tempeh, tuna, turkey	Beans, chickpeas (dried), lentils (dried), peas, soybeans
Condiments	Asian fish sauce, balsamic vinegar, capers, apple cider vinegar, Dijon mustard, marmalade, peanut butter, rice vinegar, soy sauce, strawberry jam, vanilla extract, wasabi	Barbecue sauce (check ingredients), Worcestershire sauce (check ingredients), yellow mustard
Fats	Avocado oil, butter, canola oil, coconut oil, mayonnaise, olive oil, peanut oil, sesame oil, sunflower oil, vegetable oil	
Sweeteners	Brown sugar, confectioners' sugar, dark chocolate, granulated sugar, pure maple syrup, stevia (check label for inulin, FOS, or chicory root!)	Agave nectar, honey, high-fructose corn syrup, isolmalt, maltitol, mannitol, sorbitol, xylitol
Herbs and spices	Allspice, basil, black pepper, cardamom, chipotle chile powder (not store-bought chili powder, which contains garlic; for homemade, see page 169), Chinese five-spice powder, cilantro, cinnamon, cloves, coriander seeds, cumin, curry powder (check labels for onion/garlic!), fennel seeds, fenugreek seeds, garam masala, lemongrass, mustard seeds, nutmeg, paprika, parsley, rosemary, saffron, star anise, tarragon, thyme, turmeric	Garlic powder, inulin (a.k.a. chicory root/ FOS—see sidebar for more information), onion powder
Tea	Black tea, green tea, white tea	Chamomile tea, chicory coffee, fennel tea, oolong tea

Be aware of portion sizes for the following foods, marked with an asterisk in the previous chart:

Almonds: 10 nuts or less

Avocado: ⅛ or less

Beets: 2 slices or less

Broccoli: ½ cup or less

Brussels sprouts: less than 6 sprouts

Butternut squash: ¼ cup or less

Celery: ¼ stalk or less

Chickpeas, canned: less than ¼ cup, drained

Coconut: ½ cup or less (dried, ¼ cup or less)

Corn: less than ½ cob

Cranberries, dried: 1 tablespoon or less (also currants, raisins)

Lentils, canned: less than ½ cup, drained

Pomegranate: ¼ cup seeds or less

Pumpkin, canned: ½ cup or less

Savoy cabbage: ½ cup or less

Snow peas: 5 pods or less

Sun-dried tomatoes: 2 pieces or less

Sweet potato: ½ cup or less

Check Ingredients for Common FODMAP Additives

If you are undertaking the elimination diet, you will want to read ingredient lists, because high-FODMAP ingredients sneak up in places that you would not necessarily suspect—such as gluten-free breads, sauces, and salad dressings.

Common additives that you want to look out for include agave nectar, apple or pear juice concentrate, garlic powder, high-fructose corn syrup (HFCS), honey, onion powder, and inulin (which may be disguised by other names).

Inulin is a FODMAP, part of the fructan category. It is a prebiotic fiber—meaning that it is highly fermentable food for gut bacteria. Inulin does have health benefits—but in individuals who are sensitive to it, it can cause digestive symptoms. Because inulin has a neutral taste, it is added as an ingredient to many processed foods to increase their fiber content. Check labels to see whether inulin is added to any of your foods. It is commonly found in foods advertised a "high fiber," particularly granola bars. Inulin may also be listed under the aliases chicory root, chicory root fiber, or FOS.

7-DAY ELIMINATION MEAL PLAN

You can follow this plan exactly, or make some small tweaks to the foods that you are already enjoying. These meal ideas are repeatable and interchangeable; you can swap out these meals on any day of the week. However, they are only suggestions to show you that can enjoy a wide variety of foods on an elimination diet. If you prefer, you can eat any other foods that you find in the low-FODMAP list in this chapter. Or if you love any of the meals I have suggested, feel free to continue to eat them every day (or at least until you get bored!) even after the elimination phase. And if you plow through these, and are hungry for more, you can check out my blog, www.daniellecapalino.com/blog, where I will be continuing to add new recipes!

Recipes for the meals that follow are included in chapter 7. I have made them as simple as possible—it doesn't take a chef to cook meals that will leave you feeling great.

You can make some small tweaks to make the foods that you are already enjoying work for you while you are on the elimination diet.

MONDAY

> **Breakfast:** Oatmeal with Sliced Almonds and Blueberries (113)
> **Snack:** Homemade Trail Mix (153)
> **Lunch:** Greek Salad (135) with sliced chicken
> **Snack:** Rice cake with peanut butter
> **Dinner:** Grilled salmon, Sautéed Bok Choy (141), Roasted Spiced Carrots (139)

TUESDAY

> **Breakfast:** Farm Omelet with Peppers and Spinach (115)
> **Snack:** Fruit Salad (161) and handful of almonds
> **Lunch:** Roasted Eggplant with Tahini (147) and Garden Salad (135)
> **Snack:** Popcorn sprinkled with Parmesan
> **Dinner:** Roasted Chicken Provençal with Ratatouille (124)

WEDNESDAY

> **Breakfast:** Plain lactose-free yogurt with strawberries and sliced almonds
> **Snack:** Low-FODMAP crackers (such as Mary's Gone Crackers brand) with Homemade Hummus (157)
> **Lunch:** Quinoa Salad (134) with Cinnamon Sweet Potato (149)
> **Snack:** Olives and sliced cucumbers
> **Dinner:** Vegetable Stir-fry (129) and brown rice

THURSDAY

> **Breakfast:** Chia Pudding (177)
> **Snack:** Sliced banana with almond butter
> **Lunch:** Niçoise Salad (133)
> **Snack:** Orange and Cheddar with rice cake
> **Dinner:** Coconut-Crusted Chicken (127), Spinach Sautéed with Pine Nuts (137)

FRIDAY

Breakfast: Peanut Butter Banana Smoothie (111)

Snack: Sliced turkey and almonds

Lunch: Farmhouse Frittata (123)

Snack: FODMAP-friendly snack bar (see list, page 180)

Dinner: Grilled beef fillet, Green Bean Salad 135), Rosemary Roasted Potatoes (143)

SATURDAY

Breakfast: 2 eggs scrambled with smoked salmon and chives

Snack: Sliced carrots with Homemade Hummus (157)

Lunch: Turkey sandwich with lettuce, tomato, mustard on suitable bread (see list, page 178)

Snack: Serving of gluten-free pretzels (such as Snyder's of Hanover) and 1 ounce Cheddar

Dinner: Sesame-Crusted Tuna (131), quinoa, Green Beans with Almonds (145)

SUNDAY

Breakfast: Flat Stomach French Toast (119)

Snack: Homemade Trail Mix (153)

Lunch: Garden Salad (135)

Snack: Nachos (tortilla chips with Cheddar and ⅛ avocado)

Dinner: Zucchini Noodles (151) with Basil Pesto (167)

GROCERY LIST FOR 7-DAY MEAL PLAN

This is a list of everything that you will need to follow the seven-day low-FODMAP elimination diet plan. You may be surprised to see how many of these items are already in your pantry!

The recipes, and this accompanying shopping list, have been developed to provide two servings of each dish (with a few exceptions). These recipes are so good that even your loved ones who aren't on the diet won't mind sharing them with you. Or chill the leftovers to enjoy preparation-free the next day.

FRUIT

Avocado—1

Bananas—4

Blueberries—1 pint

Cherry tomatoes—1 pint

Dried cranberries—6 ounces

Kiwis—2

Lemons—3

Oranges—2

Pineapple—1

Strawberries—1 pint

Tomatoes—4

Unsweetened coconut flakes—
one 7-ounce package

VEGETABLES

Basil—2 bunches fresh

Bell peppers—2

Bok choy—2 small heads

Broccoli—1 small head

Carrots—2 bunches

Chives—1 bunch fresh

Cucumbers—2

Dill—1 bunch fresh

Eggplants—2 large

Garlic—1 head (optional, for infused oil)

Ginger—3 inches, fresh

Green beans—two 12-ounce bags

Kale—1 bunch

Mixed lettuce—two 5-ounce packages,
or lettuce—2 heads

New potatoes—½ pound

Rosemary—1 bunch fresh, or use dried

Scallions—1 bunch (use green part only)

Spinach—one 5-ounce package, or
1 bunch

Sweet potato—1 large

Tarragon—1 bunch fresh, or use dried

Zucchini—2

PROTEIN

Beef fillets—two 4-ounce

Chicken breasts—six 4-ounce

Chickpeas—one 15-ounce can

Eggs—2 dozen large

Firm tofu—one 14-ounce package

Salmon fillets—two 4-ounce

Smoked salmon—4 ounces

Tuna—one 5-ounce can

Tuna fillets—two 4-ounce

Turkey, sliced—½ pound

DAIRY

Almond milk—1 quart

Butter, unsalted

Cheddar—½ pound

Coconut milk—one 13-ounce can

Feta cheese—4 ounces

Lactose-free milk—1 quart

Lactose-free yogurt—2 servings

Parmesan—5 ounces

NUTS AND SEEDS

Almond butter

Almonds, sliced—4 ounces

Almonds, whole—8 ounces

Chia seeds—4 ounces

Peanut butter

Pine nuts—4 ounces

Sesame seeds

Sunflower seeds—8 ounces

Tahini

GRAINS

Brown rice

Brown rice cereal—1 box, unsweetened

Gluten-free bread—1 loaf (see page 178 for suitable brands)

Gluten-free flour—4 ounces

Quinoa—12 ounces

Steel-cut oats

PANTRY

Capers

Cider vinegar

Cinnamon

Coconut oil

Coriander seeds

Garam masala

Garlic-infused oil
(for homemade, see page 154)

Granulated sugar

Grapeseed or other neutral oil

Mayonnaise

Miso paste

Mustard

Olive oil

Olives—8 ounces

Oregano

Sesame oil

Soy sauce

Unseasoned rice vinegar

Vanilla extract

SWEETS

Dark chocolate chips

Pure maple syrup

SNACKS

See page 180 for suitable brands.

Crackers

Popcorn

Pretzels

Rice cakes

Snack bar

Tortilla chips

ELIMINATION PHASE

Alexis, 32, came to see me at the suggestion of her doctor. She was three months away from her wedding and had been suffering for years with bloating and severe constipation. She had been taking the strongest prescription drugs available to deal with the constipation, but they were no longer keeping her regular. With the prescription drugs failing and her wedding dress fittings approaching, she was in a crisis.

The first GI doctor that she went to dissuaded her from trying the low-FODMAP diet because she thought it would be "too hard." This doctor clearly had not taken the time to ask Alexis what she was currently eating—if she had, she would have discovered that Alexis's diet was already way harder than the low-FODMAP diet. Her diet was limited without rhyme or reason—and on top of that, it wasn't even working. She essentially had cut out grains entirely—no rice, no quinoa, no wheat. She had also cut out nuts, because she had heard that nuts were hard to digest. In addition to wanting to get "regular," Alexis also wanted to lose weight, so she was loading up on fruits and vegetables—and she was a great cook who loved to season her food with onions and garlic.

Based on the limited diet that she was already eating, it was clear that Alexis was supermotivated and willing to make any changes necessary to feel and look good in general, and for her wedding in particular.

With my guidance and support Alexis started the elimination phase of the low-FODMAP diet, and for the first time she could remember, she started to feel great.

I helped Alexis create a diet plan that was totally low-FODMAP that she followed for several weeks. I spoke to her physician, who was amazed at the results. She had known Alexis for many years, and seen her through other nutritionists who had her on diets that seemed "healthy" but did not combat the complaints that I was addressing. Now, everyone was happy—but we were still about two months away from the wedding. Do you think that the bride-to-be wanted to start testing out foods that might bring her symptoms right back while she was inching closer to her walk down the aisle? At that point, she didn't care about figuring out exactly which of the FODMAP categories were bothering her.

Alexis wanted to wait until after she returned from her honeymoon to start testing foods, which I supported. She was more than willing to spend her honeymoon actively avoiding high-FODMAP foods if it meant that she would avoid feeling bloated and constipated—and that made sense to me, too. As soon as she came home we set up a game plan to test foods. Throughout the testing, Alexis experienced symptoms with every category. That can happen, but it was not what I had hoped! Given her history, it didn't make sense that she was going to be so sensitive to all the categories, and so I started her on some probiotics (more on probiotics on page 95). I do not like to start probiotics and the low-FODMAP diet at the same time because if you start to feel better (or worse), we will not know the cause—was it the probiotics or the diet? However, since she had already been on the low-FODMAP diet for a while, we knew that any changes at that point would be due to the probiotics.

After a few weeks of probiotic supplements, we tried the testing again, and this time Alexis was able to successfully reintroduce lactose, fructose, and sorbitol. This meant that she avoided garlic, onions, wheat, and other fructan foods, as well as beans, on an ongoing basis. Now, she will occasionally use a dietary supplement to help digest beans if she is having larger quantities of chickpeas or lentils. Alexis loved the lactose-free yogurt, so she continues to eat that, despite not having lactose intolerance. She knows that if she eats out she can order a latte, or buy a yogurt parfait and it enjoy it without worrying about her symptoms returning.

KEEP IT UP!

I know it can be tough to stick with the elimination diet, but it is worth it. Try your best to stick to it as closely as possible—but if you "cheat," don't beat yourself up. Jump back in as soon as you can and start where you left off. If you are feeling better, sticking to the plan won't be as hard as it sounds.

Another plus: While you are following the diet, you don't need to keep a diary to record everything you are eating. My experience is that my patients feel more relaxed when they are *not* keeping track of every symptom they feel and every food they eat during the elimination phase. It is helpful to keep track of your overall symptoms before and after the diet.

After two or three weeks, it's time to take inventory and see how it measured up for you. Head back to page 172 to fill out the "elimination phase" column in your symptom chart. Take a moment and be honest.

What was your score before the diet? What was your score after the elimination phase? How do your scores compare? If you have seen a drop in your score by at least 5 points, that is fantastic. Ten or more points is outstanding—now, keep it up.

THE SIMPLE METHOD: WHEN AN ELIMINATION DIET IS TOO MUCH TO BEAR

As you are reading this book, you may know deep down in your gut that the low-FODMAP diet is something that you should try—maybe because you are experiencing the symptoms that I've talked about, or because you find that you are eating a lot of high-FODMAP foods. But perhaps it's just too much to deal with because you have other things going on and not enough bandwidth to take on an elimination diet just yet. What should you do? It doesn't mean you should suffer needlessly!

Going through the elimination diet is like using a hammer, whereas the simple method is more like using a chisel—it takes a bit longer, but it can still work.

Following the simple method will take five weeks, and during that time it will be less restrictive than a full elimination diet. Each week you will exclude only one category of the FODMAPs and evaluate your symptoms. I sometimes recommend this plan for patients if there are lifestyle issues that make it difficult or impossible for them to embark on a full elimination all at once. I will also recommend this to people if after hearing their diet history, it is clear that they aren't eating all that many different FODMAPs but they are eating a disproportionate amount of one category, such as high-fructose fruits or a lot of sugar-free products. You might try this if one FODMAP category is standing out in your diet.

This is not my preferred method, as it is a little less precise, but if this is what it takes to get you going, by all means, this is better than nothing.

WEEK 1: ELIMINATE ONLY LACTOSE

Avoid: cottage cheese, cream cheese, ice cream, milk, ricotta, yogurt

WEEK 2: ELIMINATE ONLY EXCESS FRUCTOSE

Avoid: agave nectar, apples, asparagus, cherries, fresh figs, high-fructose corn syrup, honey, Jerusalem artichokes (a.k.a. sunchokes), mangoes, pears, sugar snap peas, watermelon

WEEK 3: ELIMINATE ONLY FRUCTANS

Avoid: artichokes, barley, cashews, chamomile tea, dates, dried figs, fennel tea, garlic, grapefruit, inulin (a.k.a. chicory root/FOS), leeks, onions, nectarines, oolong tea, pistachios, plums, prunes, rye, shallots, watermelon, wheat, white peaches

WEEK 4: ELIMINATE ONLY GOS

Avoid: beans, greater than ¼ cup of drained, canned chickpeas, greater than ½ cup of drained, canned lentils, peas, soybeans

WEEK 5: ELIMINATE ONLY POLYOLS

Avoid: apples, apricots, artificial sweeteners (isolmalt, maltitol, mannitol, sorbitol, xylitol), blackberries, cauliflower, mushrooms, nectarines, peaches, pears, plums, prunes, snow peas, watermelon

At the end of each week evaluate any changes to your symptoms. Notice whether your abdomen is particularly flat after avoiding each category. If you find these results after eliminating beans or lactose, for example, it may be a sign that those foods are causing your bloated abdomen. You can use the chart on page 173 to keep track from week to week.

THE SIMPLE METHOD

Whitney, 40, came to see me ostensibly because she wanted to learn more about nutrition and also to increase her energy level. Once she felt comfortable talking to me, she admitted that what she really wanted was to stop wearing workout clothes all of the time because leggings were the only pants that could fit comfortably over her waist—and she was a slim, fit woman. She was suffering from constant abdominal distention and bloating. She was also on the road traveling for work all the time, which made it hard for her to plan her meals and control every little thing she ate.

When I took a look at her three-day diet record, I found that her diet was relatively well balanced. A typical day looked like this: oatmeal with honey and coffee with milk for breakfast, an apple and almonds for a snack, a Greek salad with onions for lunch, and pasta with grilled chicken for dinner. As you might now notice, there are some high-FODMAP foods that jump right out at you: honey, milk, apple, onions, and wheat pasta.

The idea of embarking on the entire FODMAP elimination, given her lifestyle, was possible but not manageable for her. Because testing her reactions to FODMAPs seemed like the best course of action, we decided to try the simple plan instead of the full elimination diet—she should not be deprived of feeling good just because of her extensive travel. She would eliminate each of the five groups for one week at a time. This was manageable because if she was on a trip, solely focusing on avoiding lactose was doable—she could have her coffee with almond milk. Or avoiding only polyols was okay—switch her pasta for a suitable gluten-free option and avoid onions. At the end of the trial weeks Whitney felt quite confident in saying that she was reacting to both fructans and lactose. Moving forward, she found that it was manageable for her to keep up with her busy travel schedule while avoiding those foods—and eating the foods that made her feel great in her work clothes, not her workout clothes.

Testing and Creating Your Personalized Plan

THE TESTING PHASE

During the testing phase you are starting with a dietary blank slate (the low-FODMAP elimination diet) and then adding back specific high-FODMAP foods one at a time to see whether they elicit symptoms. The only way to determine which FODMAP categories cause digestive problems is to systematically test them with representative food items. Rather than staying on the elimination diet indefinitely, I want you to be able to enjoy the widest variety of foods possible, while avoiding your problematic ingredients.

FODMAPs are, generally speaking, healthy foods. It might be that only one of the categories is causing your symptoms.

You are going to be using a representative food for each category—but while you introduce that one food, try your best to keep everything else the same as when you were following the full elimination diet. This means that the only variable will be the FODMAP you are testing at that time. The foods that I suggest here are chosen because *they contain only one FODMAP*.

The testing phase is important and often overlooked. I understand that if you were terribly uncomfortable and then felt better, you wouldn't want to ever go back to feeling how you did before. However, the foods that are high in FODMAPs are, generally speaking, healthy foods. It might be that only one of the categories is causing your symptoms. It is worthwhile to figure out your culprits, so you can still enjoy the others that do not give you trouble. You don't want to go through life avoiding whole categories of food if you don't have to! (There are a few exceptions—you could healthfully go through life without high-fructose corn syrup and sugar substitutes.)

The process: You will be consuming half of a typical portion of a given food on the first test day and up to a full typical portion of the same food on the second test day. If you don't feel well after the first day, stop and do not try the food again. One possible outcome is that you tolerate the half-portion test, but not the full-portion test. If that is the case, then we will say you are moderately sensitive to that food and can tolerate smaller amounts of it going forward. This is an important outcome to note because it would indicate that you do not need to exclude that category from your diet entirely. You might even want to test some of the other foods from that category individually at a later date. If you don't feel well after any of the tests, then that doesn't mean you can never have that food again. Our tolerances to food can change over time, so you can and should revisit "failed" tests later on.

The timing: You do not need to do the tests back to back; in fact, you should wait between tests. If it seems daunting to look at the number of tests for potential food sensitivity triggers—do not worry. It might seem scary, but you can do this at your own pace. You may have a trip coming up and want to do one test before, but not want to do a test while you are away. That is totally fine. You can pick up and try these tests at any time you like. You can test one thing and then wait as long as you'd like to do another. I would encourage you to do all of the tests eventually, though, so as to not limit your diet unnecessarily.

The reason that there is a waiting period between tests is that you may need some time to clear a food out of your system. If we do not allow for adequate time—and you have a reaction—we will not know what is causing it. For that reason, even if you do not have a reaction, you should still take a small break, so that you are symptom free for at least 2 days before trying the next test.

The order: The order in which you test the categories does not matter. Often I will suggest that patients start with the category that they miss the most. If you absolutely love fruit, maybe you start with fructose. On the other hand, you might have a hunch that a certain category is causing symptoms for you, and want to start with that. I have put the tests in an order that I find works well, but go in any order that you would like.

There is one caveat to my flexibility on order. Within the *fructan* test, try wheat *last*, after garlic and onion. Because garlic, onion, and wheat are all in the fructan category, if we isolate wheat, we can use the wheat test as a proxy to evaluate tolerance of gluten. If you do not react to garlic or onion, but you do not tolerate wheat, it could suggest a gluten sensitivity rather than a FODMAP sensitivity. If you react to more than one of the fructan tests, it would suggest a FODMAP sensitivity, giving you the flexibility not to worry about gluten contamination.

Follow this chart during the testing phase:

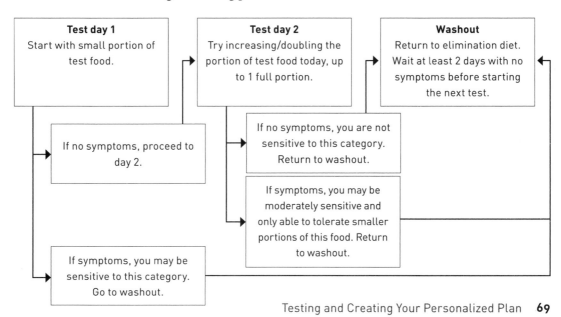

Take the Tests

Use the chart on page 173 to track your reactions to each test.

The polyol category encompasses two food subcategories—sorbitol and mannitol. My philosophy is always, "Why avoid foods that you don't have to?" so, the benefit of breaking polyols down into sorbitol and mannitol for the testing phase means narrowing down bothersome bloating foods. If you were not already eating artificial sweeteners, you do not need to test them. If you were eating a significant amount of artificial sweeteners, you may wish to test those separately—but even if they don't bother you, I do not recommend including high-FODMAP artificial sweeteners in a healthy-gut diet.

I've separated out the different types of fructans—garlic, onion, wheat—into individual tests. You may find that you react differently to each of these.

TEST 1A—POLYOLS (SORBITOL)

Try blackberries. Sorbitol is used an artificial sweetener and is also a natural component of foods. A good food choice to test tolerance to sorbitol is blackberries. Start with a small portion of five blackberries, and, if tolerated, try up to ten on day two.

TEST 1B—POLYOLS (MANNITOL)

Try mushrooms. If you hate mushrooms, you can substitute cauliflower (cooked or raw, but cooked will be easier to digest) for this test. Start test day one with ¼ cup of mushrooms (cooked or raw); if tolerated, increase to up to ½ cup on day two.

TEST 2—LACTOSE

Try regular milk. To test tolerance to lactose, regular milk is a good choice. If you hate milk, you can use plain yogurt as a substitute. Start with ½ cup on test day one. If you do not have symptoms, increase to 1 cup on day two.

TEST 3—FRUCTOSE

Try honey. Start the fructose test with 1 to 2 teaspoons of honey. You can eat it off a spoon, or add it to a low-FODMAP tea (green tea, perhaps). If test day one is successful, increase to 1 to 2 tablespoons on day two.

TEST 4—FRUCTANS

Try garlic. Start this test by adding ½ clove of garlic to your otherwise low-FODMAP foods. If tolerated, increase to one to two cloves of garlic on day two.

TEST 4B—FRUCTANS

Try onions. Try adding 2 tablespoons to ¼ cup of onions on test day one. If tolerated, increase to up to ½ cup on day two.

TEST 4C—FRUCTANS

Try bread. Try one piece of bread made of wheat (white or wholegrain) on test day one and if tolerated increase to two slices on day two. Try a bread that does not contain other common FODMAP ingredients, such as honey.

> ### Is It the Gluten?
> Testing bread that is made of wheat is a makeshift way to assess gluten sensitivity. If you find that you are not reacting to garlic or onions but you do react to wheat, it may suggest sensitivity to gluten rather than sensitivity to fructans. On the other hand, if you thought that you had a gluten sensitivity but you find yourself reacting to other fructans, then you may not actually have a gluten sensitivity after all—and it might be FODMAPs that you are reacting to.

TEST 5—GOS

Try black beans. Finally, try ¼ cup of black beans and if tolerated increase to ½ cup on day two.

THE PERSONALIZATION PHASE: WHAT TO EAT NOW THAT YOU HAVE IDENTIFIED YOUR TRIGGERS

Now that you have figured out which of the FODMAP categories are making you feel unwell, it's time to learn what to do about it—and you can start right now.

Sorbitol

If you tolerated the sorbitol test, you can eat foods that are high in sorbitol, noting that there can be overlap with other categories.

SORBITOL

Apples (also have fructose), apricots (also have fructans), avocados, blackberries, broccoli (large quantities also have fructans and GOS), nectarines (also have fructans), pears (also have fructose), plums (also have fructans), prunes (also have fructans), sweet corn (also has GOS), white peaches (also have fructans), yellow peaches

Mannitol

If you tolerated the mannitol test, you can add back these foods— and potentially watermelon, pending the results of the fructan and fructose tests.

MANNITOL

Cauliflower, mushrooms, snow peas, watermelon (also has fructans and fructose)

If you did not eat foods using high-FODMAP artificial sweeteners prior to the elimination diet, I would not start including them now. You can assess your tolerance to foods containing polyol sweeteners and decide how to proceed.

Lactose

If you found that you were sensitive to lactose, do not fret, as this does not mean that you cannot eat dairy. You have a few options here—luckily, there are many lactose-free dairy products. For example, you can purchase lactose-free milk, lactose-free yogurt, even lactose-free ice cream! Some people are able to even tolerate Greek yogurt. Hard cheeses are okay, too—that includes such things as Parmesan and Cheddar. One trick you can use to tell if a cheese has lactose is to look at the nutrition facts label under "carbohydrates"—and if it lists 0, then you are good to go (because lactose is a type of sugar, or carbohydrate).

If you found that you are *not* sensitive to lactose you can incorporate all dairy products into your diet.

LACTOSE

High: condensed milk (used in such items as Thai iced tea), cottage cheese, cream cheese, ice cream, milk, yogurt, ricotta

Low: butter, feta, Cheddar, Parmesan, Swiss, as well as *lactose-free* cottage cheese, cream cheese, milk, yogurt

Lactose Tips

- Lactose-free does not mean dairy-free: you can still enjoy hard cheeses and butter.

- You can try taking a lactase enzyme to help your body break down lactose in dishes that contain lactose.

- You may be able to tolerate some lactose. One guideline is trying to stay under 4 grams of lactose per meal or snack. What does 4 grams of lactose look like?

  - Less than ½ cup of cottage cheese

  - Less than ¼ of cup milk

  - About 2 tablespoons of yogurt

  - About 2 tablespoons of cream cheese

- Remember there are low-lactose dairy options: butter, Cheddar, kefir, Parmesan, Swiss—not to mention any dairy labeled "lactose-free"!

- Many excellent dairy-free alternatives are lactose-free (be sure to check labels for sweeteners or soy if fructose or GOS are issues for you).

Fructose

If you found out that you are sensitive to fructose, portion control on fruits will be key. Unfortunately, it is the case that fruits are a main source of excess fructose in your diet. And, of course, fruit is part of a healthy diet. But there are plenty of fruits that are not high in excess fructose, so those will become your staples. The other main sources of fructose are honey, agave nectar, and high-fructose corn syrup, and you don't really want much if any of those in your diet anyway. Don't be fooled into thinking that agave is healthy—it is sugar masquerading as a healthy alternative.

If you found that you are not sensitive to fructose, you can incorporate fructose foods into your diet.

....

FRUCTOSE

Agave nectar, apples, asparagus, cherries, figs, honey, high-fructose corn syrup, Jerusalem artichokes (a.k.a. sunchokes), mangoes, pears, watermelon

Tips for Low-Fructose Living

- Replace honey or agave with pure maple syrup as a sweetener in such things as oatmeal.

- Stock up on low-FODMAP fruits, such as bananas, oranges, melon, and pineapple.

- Enjoy fruit one serving at a time—even though it's healthy, it can potentially make you bloated should you eat more.

....

Fructose Absorption and Glucose

To get into the specifics here, it is technically not fructose that is the culprit—it is fructose *in excess of glucose*. Huh? Your body uses glucose to help usher fructose in for absorption. When there are equal amounts of fructose and glucose, then there is no problem absorbing the fructose. But when a food has more fructose then glucose, you run out of glucose to help bring in the fructose—and end up with leftover fructose that is not broken down. While this happens to everyone, some people are particularly sensitive to this excess. All of the lists of low-FODMAP fruits that I have provided contain equal ratios of fructose and glucose, so you should not experience any discomfort when enjoying them.

You may be asking yourself whether there is any way to actually get extra glucose to help shuttle in the rest of the fructose. Scientists are asking the same question. While research thus far shows that glucose does help in the absorption of fructose, it does not help prevent symptoms from the fructose malabsorption. The takeaway: Adding glucose to your diet will not help prevent symptoms of fructose malabsorption.

Fructans

So, you are sensitive to fructans . . . this category is honestly the most complicated because the things in here are admittedly hardest to avoid. *You may not be sensitive to everything here, which is why we tested onions, garlic, and wheat separately.*

If you are sensitive to garlic, you can still enjoy garlic-infused oil (for homemade, see page 154).

If you are sensitive to onions, you can try chives, or the green part of scallions, and the green part of leeks for similar flavors.

If you are sensitive to wheat, you can still have gluten-free options for breads, pastas, and the like, made of rice, corn, and quinoa, among others.

If you did not experience symptoms, then you can go back to these foods.

....

FRUCTANS

Barley, cashews, chamomile tea, dates, dried figs, fennel tea, garlic, inulin (a.k.a. chicory root/FOS), leeks, nectarines, onions, oolong tea, pistachios, plums, prunes, rye, shallots, watermelon, wheat, white peaches

....

GOS

So, you are sensitive to GOS . . . but it doesn't mean bye-bye beans entirely. You can still enjoy small portions of canned chickpeas and canned lentils. It would be a shame to exclude these from your diet since they are terrific, affordable, tolerable sources of important dietary fiber and protein.

You can still have drained, canned:

Chickpeas: less than ¼ cup—this seems like a tiny amount, but still counts. It means you can enjoy homemade hummus or some chickpeas tossed into a salad.

Lentils: less than ½ cup—this could be a homemade lentil soup!

If you did not experience symptoms in your testing, you can go back to eating these foods.

GOS

Beans, lentils, peas, soybeans

What About Foods That Are in More Than One Group?

Although you have completed the six simple tests, a few foods still remain that you are avoiding and have not tested.

- If you tolerated both **fructose** and **sorbitol**: You should be able to enjoy apples, cherries, and pears. As with the other tests, start with ½ portion (such as half a piece of fruit, or about 3 cherries) before trying larger amounts.
- If you tolerated both **fructans** and **sorbitol**: You should be able to enjoy nectarines, white peaches and plums. As with the other tests, start with ½ portion (such as half a piece of fruit) before trying larger amounts.
- If you tolerated **fructans**, **fructose,** and **mannitol**: You should be able to enjoy watermelon. Start with ¼ slice to test it out.

Foods That Are Not Listed

As the research on FODMAP content of foods is still evolving, there may be some foods that you do not find listed. If there are other foods that you have not yet tested, use the same method as for those that are: Start with half a typical portion to assess symptoms, and if you do not experience symptoms after day one, increase up to one full portion on day two. If you tolerate a small or full portion of the food, you may incorporate into your diet.

Tolerances May Change

Keep note of any foods that bother you throughout the testing phase. Your tolerances may change over time, so although a food may bother you now, you may be able to test it again later.

The Importance of Testing Foods

If the elimination diet works for you, you will likely find yourself in a situation where you not only have no desire to try to reintroduce foods, but you actually might be afraid to try—for fear of eliciting the symptoms that you once had. I understand the fear, and the concept of feeling great and not wanting to screw it up. However, as a dietitian it doesn't feel right for me to just say, okay—avoid apples for the rest of your life, or no more asparagus or garlic for you, without having real evidence that you should avoid those foods.

Getting people to let go of the fear of reintroduction is one of the hardest things that I have to overcome with my patients. It is also the reason that following along on this journey without a dietitian can be challenging. You need someone to hold you accountable and force you to really challenge yourself. Let me be your coach—I want the best for you. My big goal is for you to end up having the most varied diet possible while also maintaining your healthy gut and flat stomach!

WHAT DO I DO, NOW THAT I HAVE FIGURED OUT WHAT'S BOTHERING ME?

You may be wondering, now that you have discovered which foods you need to avoid, whether you need to avoid them forever. The answer is no and yes. Essentially, things change. Food allergies aside (please do not try to eat something that you are truly allergic to!), when we are talking about food sensitivities, our body is in constant flux. It's not quite "lactose intolerant today, gone tomorrow," but you may have developed your sensitivities as a result of a food-borne illness, and it may take a while (months, years) for your system to fully recover. And then you may find you can go back to, say, lactose after avoiding it for so long. For that reason, I

> **Allergies vs. Sensitivities**
> **Food allergies** can be very serious or life threatening and can occur from ingesting or inhaling miniscule amounts of a food substance. Food allergies will always elicit a reaction.
> **Food sensitivities** are not life threatening, and are usually limited to digestive consequences. Typically, they will occur only when eating a food frequently and in significant quantity.

would suggest not writing off any food indefinitely (unless, again, you are allergic, then obviously *avoid avoid avoid*).

WHAT IF I'M VEGETARIAN OR VEGAN?

Not going to lie: Being a vegetarian or vegan on the low-FODMAP diet is more complicated, because you can't rely on animal-based protein sources, such as meat or fish, and because you are limited in vegetarian protein staples, such as beans—but it is possible. As you know foods that are all protein (e.g., meat, egg) do not contain carbohydrates and thus do not contain FODMAPs. But this does not mean that a vegetarian or vegan low-FODMAP diet is not possible. It will just take a little bit of extra work to make sure that you are getting all the nutrients you need while you embark on this elimination diet.

SAMPLE VEGETARIAN MEAL PLAN

Breakfast: Scrambled eggs with spinach, roasted sweet potato
Snack: String cheese and an orange
Lunch: Salad with ¼ cup of drained, canned chickpeas; carrots; cucumber; tomato; and oil and vinegar or a low-FODMAP dressing (for homemade, see pages 163–65)
Snack: Lactose-free yogurt and strawberries
Dinner: Vegetable stir-fry with tofu

Suitable Vegetarian Protein Sources

Buckwheat, chickpeas (canned), cornmeal, eggs, firm tofu, hard cheeses (lactose-free), lactose-free milk, lentils (canned), quinoa, tempeh

SAMPLE VEGAN MEAL PLAN

Breakfast: Oatmeal with chia seeds, and blueberries
Snack: 10 olives and 15 gluten-free, whole-grain crackers (such as Mary's Gone Crackers brand)
Lunch: Salad with ¼ cup of drained, canned chickpeas, carrots, cucumber, tomato, and oil and vinegar or a low-FODMAP dressing (for homemade, see pages 163–65)

Snack: Orange and gluten-free pretzels (such as Snyder's of Hanover brand)

Dinner: Vegetable stir-fry with tofu

Suitable Vegan Protein Sources

Buckwheat, chickpeas (canned), cornmeal, dairy-free cheeses (check label for soy and sweeteners), dairy-free milk (check label for soy and sweeteners), dairy-free yogurt (check label for soy and sweeteners), firm tofu, lentils (canned), quinoa, tempeh

VEGETARIAN

Sasha, age 28, came to me to help get her on the low-FODMAP diet to combat the diarrhea she had been suffering from as long as she could remember. She was a lifelong vegetarian for ethical reasons—and was afraid that she wouldn't be able to get the nutrients she needed by being both a vegetarian and on the low-FODMAP diet. I reassured her that the elimination phase is only temporary and that she would likely be able to add back certain food groups once she determined her tolerance to those foods.

Even if she did have stay on a strict low-FODMAP diet, I told her that I am the queen of finding foods that you *can* eat—even if she did have to avoid certain categories. Despite having strong convictions about her vegetarianism, she was actually contemplating eating meat because she was so afraid of becoming malnourished. I didn't want her to have to compromise her ethical integrity to feel good. If you work with a seasoned professional, there are ways to make this diet work for you, even with other dietary limitations, such as vegetarianism.

Like many vegetarians, Sasha had become reliant on beans as a protein source. She also enjoyed Greek yogurt and eggs. Sasha liked cooking and, because of her work schedule, she devoted two days a week to preparing larger batches of food that she could then enjoy throughout the week. In her three-day diet record I found that a typical day for her would include a frittata of eggs with peppers, onions, and potatoes for breakfast; a sandwich with hummus, cheese, roasted mushrooms, and eggplant for lunch; berries and cashews for a snack; and a stir-fry for dinner with carrots, green beans, and sugar snap peas on a bed of brown rice. Because she cooked batches of the items that were staples in her diet, these same dishes recurred throughout the week.

For the elimination diet she had limited portions of legumes and still ate nuts and seeds—but replaced the cashews with walnuts, and added sliced almonds to her stir-fry. She tried a coconut milk yogurt to replace the Greek yogurt that she liked while maintaining a similar taste and consistency. She made her own hummus to use as a spread on sandwiches, and also as a dip for vegetables and crackers.

When we met for a follow-up three weeks later, Sasha was overjoyed. By making these tweaks to her diet, she felt great and felt empowered to know what food choices to make to keep feeling great. Together we created a plan going forward that included limited portions of legumes, lots of nuts and seeds, and some eggs and hard cheeses. Sasha was very happy to be able to maintain the vegetarian lifestyle that she chose, while knowing that she could get the nutrients she needed, and maintain her digestive health.

Other Factors Affecting Your Gut

The low-FODMAP diet removes the most common dietary culprits that could be at the root of your upset digestive system. But there are some other factors that might be at play. The following list includes some other factors beyond FODMAPs that can contribute to digestive ailments. Scan the list—use your intuition here—to see whether any of these things stick out for you. (For example, are you drinking a large bottle of carbonated water every day and suffering from reflux? Are your symptoms at their worst after a night of too much alcohol?) You might want to pick one that makes sense for you and try it alongside, or after, the elimination diet.

High-Fat/Fried Foods
Even though fat is not a FODMAP, it does not mean you are going to be home free with home fries. Fatty and fried foods can slow down your digestion and can cause digestive upset and bloating as well.

Caffeine
Caffeine acts as a stimulant and can speed up your digestive tract. It can be an irritant and cause digestive upsets and urgent bathroom runs.

Alcohol
Even one drink can disturb your digestion by causing such problems as heartburn or diarrhea.

Carbonation

The bubbles in your soda or sparkling water fill your stomach with excess air when you swallow them. It can cause bloating, burping, and acid reflux.

Gum

Along the same lines as carbonation, gum introduces excess air into your digestive system because of how we breathe and swallow while chewing gum. For some individuals, chewing gum can cause bloating, burping, and acid reflux.

Dairy

There is often a lot of confusion around dairy. The low-FODMAP diet is *not a dairy-free diet*; it is a low-lactose diet in the elimination phase, and in the personalization phase *if* you are lactose intolerant. After you have finished the testing phase, you will determine whether you are lactose intolerant. If you are not lactose intolerant, you will be able to enjoy any dairy product you wish. If you are lactose intolerant, then you can enjoy lactose-free dairy products.

Having said that, I do believe that there is a difference between a laboratory result suggesting that mozzarella is very low in lactose and a person enjoying a mozzarella pizza. This is where my clinical expertise sheds light on the data. Despite low-lactose levels, the majority of my lactose intolerant patients do not tolerate mozzarella or Camembert, whereas Parmesan is tolerated well. I have taken this into consideration in compiling the recipes that I share with you in this book. But follow your own instincts on this as well—trust your guts.

Some dairy products simply cannot be replaced with lactose-free alternatives—but it may not mean that you need to avoid them entirely. Lactase supplements will break down lactose into component parts making it easier to digest for people who are lactose intolerant. If you find that you are intolerant to lactose, you may want to experiment with a lactase supplement to see whether it helps you enjoy certain foods without symptoms arising. Or try out nondairy alternatives (check label for soy and sweeteners) to see whether you like them.

What Is Milk Made Of?

Whole milk is made of:

Fat (3–4%)
Protein (3.5%)
Lactose (5%)
Water (87%)

LACTOSE

Matthew, age 55, is a successful businessman who came in to my office wearing a suit and tie. His doctor had recommended that he come see me because he had nothing left to offer after the extensive testing, including endoscopies and colonoscopies had found nothing wrong, and yet Matthew was complaining that he had acid reflux and abdominal cramps that were sending him to the bathroom in embarrassment at work. In fact, he had just left an appointment with his gastroenterologist when he came to see me the first time. Diet was not the first thing that he tried to help alleviate his symptoms—he had spent the past few months rotating through antispasmodic and antacid medications to no avail.

Matthew was really suffering from these symptoms and was frustrated that the medical route had failed him. He lived about 45 minutes from Manhattan and sometimes he would have to pull over on the road during his commute to the city, to use a bathroom. He had memorized where all of the clean bathrooms were on his route. The last thing anyone wants to do is fear having this kind of accident on the road, when one is concerned enough about the traffic and making it to work on time. He was miserable and desperate.

When it came time to sit down together to look at what he was currently eating, I found that he had a pretty limited diet already—self-limited in an attempt to try to rid his diet of things that bothered him. He ate rice crackers with cottage cheese every morning with a latte, a bagel and cream cheese in the afternoon. To try to alleviate the taste and discomfort of the bitterness in his mouth, he would go through a pack of gum every day. Looking at his diet, it jumped out at me that he was eating a significant amount of dairy as well as chewing gum containing a substantial amount of artificial sweeteners.

Based on these eating habits, I identified two FODMAP categories that really stood out: lactose and polyols from all of his sugar-free gum. Matthew was set in his ways but also desperate for relief. He was very open to the idea of making any changes that I suggested. In his case, I was not worried about cutting out bread. When I am working one-on-one with patients, I am able to get a sense of people's reactions to my suggestions. My hunch was that the lactose and artificial sweeteners were a bigger issue for Matthew than the bread. Lucky for both of us, I was correct.

I suggested two big changes to his diet—for him to (1) switch over to lactose-free dairy products, and (2) stop chewing gum. I worked with him to find some alternatives that he would enjoy. He bought lactose-free yogurt, lactose-free cream cheese, and some mints that were made with real sugar. I found with Matthew, and I see this frequently, that he really enjoyed going grocery shopping for new products—it can give a sense of empowerment.

Matthew came back to my office a week later, saying that he was feeling great—no longer feeling the burning and experiencing the bad taste in his mouth. He didn't even end up trying the mints that he bought because there was no need, since he no longer experienced the bitter acidic taste that he had been complaining of. He called me a week later when he realized he was no longer stopping on his commute to work. These small low-FODMAP adjustments completely changed his life and he did not even view them as a big compromise. He did not miss the dairy, since he swapped in the lactose-free variety.

Something else that I had noticed about Matthew was he was not eating very much—if any—fruit. We did end up working on increasing fruit and vegetable intake in subsequent meetings, but our initial focus was on symptom alleviation. I find people are more willing to make other changes to their diet once they start to feel better.

Gluten

Gluten is a protein found in wheat, barley, and rye. People with celiac disease need to avoid gluten, but there may be other people with non-celiac gluten sensitivity who need to avoid it as well.

Other Artificial Sweeteners

If you are reading really carefully, you might notice that some artificial sweeteners are not on the "no" list. That doesn't mean that I think they are a safe choice. Even though they might be low-FODMAP, it doesn't mean that they are not causing you any problems.

How Do I Make Sure I am Getting Enough Fiber?

One of the things that you want to be mindful of is making sure that you get enough fiber. This is especially true if you suffer from constipation. You need to be mindful of fiber because you can easily miss out on it when you cut out certain fruits, vegetables, and grains during the elimination phase of the low-FODMAP diet. Focus on low-FODMAP and easy-to-digest sources of fiber:

Blueberries (¾ cup)	1.2 grams fiber
Carrots (½ cup)	2 grams fiber
Chia seeds (1 tablespoon)	5.2 grams fiber
Oatmeal (½ cup cooked)	2 grams fiber
Papaya (½ cup)	1.2 grams fiber
Quinoa (½ cup cooked)	2.5 grams fiber
Spinach (½ cup)	1.6 grams fiber
Sweet potato (½ cup)	4 grams fiber
Winter squash (½ cup)	1 gram fiber

HOW MUCH FIBER SHOULD I BE EATING PER DAY?

Men 50 or younger	38 grams
Men 51 or older	30 grams
Women 50 or younger	25 grams
Women 51 or older	21 grams

What about Calcium?

If you exclude dairy altogether, you may not be getting enough calcium in your diet. However, you can enjoy plenty of lactose-free dairy options that are good sources of calcium, even if you are lactose intolerant. For instance, remember that you can have lactose-free milk, lactose-free yogurt, even lactose-free cream cheese. If dairy is not a part of your diet and you want to make sure you are getting enough calcium, there are also some great low-FODMAP dairy-free sources of calcium, including oatmeal, leafy greens (such as collards and spinach), firm tofu, canned salmon, and sardines.

Beans

I believe that beans are a key part of a healthy diet. At the same time, we know that eating a lot of beans can cause uncomfortable gas in just about anyone. We don't want to avoid beans entirely, because they have incredible health benefits and are a great source of protein and fiber. So, how can you eat beans and maintain a flat stomach and healthy gut? During the elimination phase of the diet, and even if you find in the testing phase that you are sensitive to GOS, you can still enjoy smaller portions of canned lentils and canned chickpeas. This is a whole lot more convenient than cooking beans yourself, which takes forever. How did you get so lucky that you have a pass on cooking beans? Well, the GOS portion of the beans loves water—and it seeps into the water, out of the bean. Because canned beans hang out on the shelves, the water gets full of the GOS and when you drain the can, you pour out most of the GOS along with the liquid! Rinse the beans and you lose even more of the GOS.

Similar to lactase supplements available to help with digestion of lactose, you can purchase alpha-galactosidase enzyme supplements (such as Beano) to aid with the digestion of beans. Unlike lactase, which the body normally does produce, we do not produce the enzyme that breaks down beans. Although we do not produce this enzyme, not everyone who eats beans feels unwell as a result. Some people are naturally more sensitive to the effects of poorly digested bean fibers than others. One potential way to mitigate the uncomfortable effects that you may feel from eating beans is to take a supplement with your food.

Chickpeas and Lentils

Reminder—on the elimination diet, and if you find that you are sensitive to GOS, you can still enjoy:

Chickpeas: less than ¼ cup, canned, drained, and rinsed

Lentils: less than ½ cup, canned, drained, and rinsed

Garlic

Why on earth can you eat garlic-infused oil, but not garlic, garlic powder, garlic paste, and so on? Please join me on a little trip back to high school biology, where we learned about solubility. The FODMAP part of the garlic, the fructans, is water soluble, not fat-soluble. This means that when you put the garlic in a fat (such as oil), the FODMAP part does not go into the fat. However, since it is water-soluble, if you are making a stock or soup that is water-based, then the FODMAP part does leach out into the water.

The good news—in terms of spicing up your dietary repertoire—is that you can use garlic- or onion-infused oil. You have two options: you can either make it at home (page 154) or buy it. One thing to keep in mind is that if you make it at home, you should use it for the recipe you are making, but it is not safe to store home-infused oils.

What's Up with Soy?

There is also some confusion around soy—understandably so, because technically, soybeans are high-FODMAP, and yet some products made from soybeans are not! For example, firm tofu is a great plant-based protein source. Tofu is made from soybeans, but during the process of making tofu, the fructans leach out and you are left with a versatile food product that is low-FODMAP. Similarly, tempeh is made of soybeans, but it is fermented and the fermentation process renders it low-FODMAP. Soy milk can be made from either soybeans or soy protein. If soy milk is made from soybeans, it is not low-FODMAP. However, soy milk that is made from soy protein is suitable for the elimination diet. The only company that I am aware of at this time that makes milk from soy protein is 8th Continent. In all honesty, it is probably easier to leave off soy milk altogether for the elimination phase.

AUTOIMMUNE

Betsy, age 35, wearing loose jogging pants and a blousy top, walked into my office, complaining of severe bloating and distention. Her presentation was remarkable: Despite her slimness, her abdomen was rounded and distended. She was a fashionable woman and was upset to explain to me that the pants she was wearing were the only ones she could comfortably wear due to her condition. She had a significant medical history and a rare autoimmune disease that sent her all the way to the Mayo Clinic to seek a specialist. She would continue to fly to the Mayo Clinic regularly for continued care. Because of her condition, she had been worked up extensively and had been tested for celiac disease and other potential medical explanations for her gastrointestinal ailments. She did not test positive for celiac disease, and her doctors had been discouraging about the potential of gluten or any other food to be causing her continued symptoms.

Despite discouragement from her doctors about the impact of dietary changes, Betsy came to see me for my professional opinion. I tend not to start with a gluten-free diet for patients without a celiac diagnosis. However, it was unusual to see a patient with other severe autoimmune conditions. Knowing that celiac disease is an autoimmune condition and that having autoimmune conditions predisposes you to others, I felt that this situation warranted a gluten-free experiment.

In her case, Betsy was willing to jump right into gluten-free and I felt that was enough of a change to get her started. We started off on just a gluten-free diet and the results were incredible. She came back to see me two weeks later and I could see a dramatic difference in her appearance. I spoke to her doctors at the Mayo Clinic and they could not believe how significantly her change in diet had affected her symptoms and her physical presentation.

Even though going gluten-free was very helpful, it resolved only about 80 percent of her symptoms. As a practitioner I have seen many people who thought that they were gluten sensitive, but actually turned out to need the low-FODMAP diet instead of a gluten-free diet. In Betsy's case, it seemed that a combination was needed to fully help her. I went through the three-day diet record that she kept and highlighted the high-FODMAP foods and suggested changes for her. While I tried to make the diet as easy as possible to follow, Betsy was so happy with the initial results that she was just as happy to cut out certain foods entirely (such as apples, asparagus, and garlic) and did not feel that she wanted replacements. Having gone through difficult medical problems for much of her life, she now had an outlook that was optimistic and encouraged: She was grateful for the improvement she saw and felt that giving up certain foods was a small sacrifice to make.

When I guided her through the testing

phase, we found that Betsy reacted to garlic and excess fructose as well. Once we layered on the gluten-free and low-FODMAP, she was about 95 percent better than when she started (not everyone will feel 100 percent better, but she was thrilled by this result). She did an awesome job managing her food sensitivities without feeling deprived. Instead, she felt empowered and finally put her dress pants back on.

What about Probiotics?

Probiotics are a total buzzword at the moment. By definition, probiotics are live bacteria that, when given in sufficient quantity, confer health benefits. It may be a bit creepy at first to think of probiotics as what they actually are, but they do a tremendous amount of good for you. There is tons of emerging research about probiotics—and one of the main areas of study is in digestive health.

Probiotics can help with a whole host of gastrointestinal complaints. You may want to try one yourself. Besides buying supplements, one way to get the incredible health benefits of probiotics is to make them a part of your diet. We get probiotics through food that has been fermented. You can enjoy some fermented foods on the elimination phase of the diet, and also in the long-term personalized phase. Some of the best probiotic-rich foods that you enjoy on this diet are lactose-free yogurt and kefir. Don't like dairy? I have included some recipes to use miso, which is a savory fermented soy product. Also, remember that nondairy yogurt (check labels for soy and sweeteners) will also provide the kinds of probiotics found in dairy yogurt. Kombucha is another good source of probiotics (just be sure to check for high-FODMP ingredients like mango and sweeteners).

Eating Out and Low-FODMAP Ready-Made

How the heck do I follow this diet? Tips to get through the elimination phase

Surely, even with all of this information, some questions are going to arise about how to make this elimination diet practical and doable—even when you're not cooking for yourself.

HOW TO EAT OUT LOW-FODMAP

If you know where you are going, you can plan ahead. You might want to look online to check out the menu of the restaurant you are going to. If you don't have a chance to do that, you can look here for ideas and also for things to watch for when dining on particular types of cuisine.

Say lunch was brought in for a meeting and you don't get to order to your liking. There is usually a green salad, and you can pick out the onions. If there is a sandwich with turkey or tuna salad, eat the middle and skip the bread. You'll even be safe having some potato chips.

Say you are going out on a date, maybe it's a blind date, or maybe it's a special anniversary. Whatever the case, you don't want to be running to the bathroom after the first course (well, unless it's a bad blind date!!).

Other Dining Situations

French: Order a simply grilled fish or chicken paillard with a side of rice and steamed vegetables, such as carrots, green beans, eggplant, and zucchini. *Things to be aware of:* garlic! Ask your server whether your food can be prepared without spices. You can even ask that the bread basket be removed so that you aren't tempted.

Indian: Grilled chicken and rice; dosa with potato. *Things to be aware of:* garlic, onion, and sauces. *Pro tip:* If you are traveling in India, you can seek out establishments that are more religiously observant (Hindu or Jain) as these cultures do not eat onion or garlic for religious reasons.

Italian: Try arugula salad with shaved Parmesan, balsamic vinegar, and olive oil; grilled or roasted chicken with roasted potatoes and zucchini; shrimp cocktail; polenta; Simply grilled fish with side of eggplant or spinach; for dessert, sorbet. *Things to be aware of:* garlic! Also, watch out for other ingredients in gluten-free pasta dishes (remember gluten-free does not necessarily equal FODMAP-free).

Japanese: Green salad; miso soup; almost any sushi rolls—try to limit to two rolls. You want to avoid large amounts of avocado if you are in the elimination phase of the diet. One avocado roll is okay, but if you are having another roll, try tuna, salmon, or yellowtail and cucumber. *Things to be aware of:* If you are following a gluten-free diet, California rolls are not a good choice as the imitation crabmeat contains gluten. Also soy sauce is okay for the low-FODMAP diet, but it does contain gluten. A popular brand of reduced-sodium soy sauce also contains lactose, so be mindful of reading labels. Call ahead and ask or bring your own gluten-free soy sauce or tamari.

Mexican: Enchilada with chicken, beef, or pork; tacos with lettuce, cheese, beef, or chicken; tortilla chips; fajita with meat, peppers, rice, tomatoes. *Things to be aware of:* onions! The good news is that you can typically see the onions in Mexican food—and you might be okay by removing them from the dish.

Steak house: Try lean cuts of beef; a 4- to 6-ounce steak with ½ baked potato and steamed spinach or green beans. Or lobster, if it's surf and turf night. *Things to be aware of:* Remember that although beef is a protein and totally low-FODMAP, some cuts are very fatty and the fattiness can also cause or exacerbate GI symptoms. Also, steaks may be marinated in high-FODMAP ingredients prior to cooking, so ask your server before you order. Hamburger meat may be mixed with onion and garlic, so be sure to ask about that as well.

Thai: Stir-fry and steamed vegetables, rice or rice noodles with tofu, fish, shrimp, chicken, beef, or pork; chicken satay. *Things to be aware of:* garlic, onion, and unknown ingredients in general, such as in sauces. Ask your server whether you can be served a sauce that is free of dairy, onion, and garlic.

Here are some general awareness tips for eating out:

- Salad dressings are tricky as they almost always contain onion and garlic—and sometimes lactose—so stick with oil and vinegar in a restaurant.
- Sauces are often an unknown entity. Don't be afraid to ask for sauce on the side, or to ask your server what the ingredients are so you can determine whether it will work for you.
- Look up a menu in advance, if possible. Pick out what you think might work for you. Call ahead to the restaurant during off-peak hours to discuss your dietary restrictions and see whether they can be accommodated.

HOW TO TRAVEL LOW-FODMAP

It can definitely pay off to do some research about the place you are traveling to before takeoff. There are always suitable options to order in a restaurant, and if you have access to a kitchen or a fridge in your hotel room, of course you can stop by a local grocery store and load up on foods you are comfortable eating while you are away.

The two big issues that come up while traveling are eating out and airplane, car, and on-the-go snacks.

Airplane and Car Snacks

The following is a list of snacks that you can pack and bring onto an airplane or in the car for a long journey.

- Fruits and vegetables: bananas, blueberries, clementines, grapes, oranges, pineapple (cut up), strawberries
- Dairy: lactose-free yogurt, string cheese
- Hard-boiled eggs, olives
- Oatmeal packets that you can make with hot water (bonus points if you bring a baggie with toppings for the oatmeal—or buy in advance, such as bringing mini packets of chia seeds)
- Snack foods: gluten-free pretzels (such as Snyder's of Hanover), tortilla chips, potato chips, your own trail mix (page 153)

On the Go Bars

Finding prepackaged snacks on the go can be tricky for anyone— let alone if you are on the elimination phase of this diet. To save the hassle of buying things on the go, stock up on your favorite bars to carry with you, once you decide which one is your favorite. Although these bars haven't necessarily been tested in a lab, my patients enjoy them comfortably.

- GoMacro MacroBar Protein Replenishment, Peanut Butter
- KIND granola bars—not to be confused with other KIND bars, these are square shaped. Although these do contain honey, it is used in a small-enough quantity that my patients usually do well with these—and they are easy to find in stores.
- Nicer Foods Be Nice Bars

Gut-Friendly Recipes

You do not need to be a chef to follow the elimination phase of the low-FODMAP diet. However, if you cook—or want some ideas of ingredient combinations that would be suitable for the diet—I have included a collection of recipes that my patients and I enjoy. The following are simple and easy recipes for the basic items you need to adapt to fit into the low-FODMAP diet. All of these recipes are gluten-free, or can easily be made gluten-free by using tamari instead of soy sauce. Most of these recipes accommodate the seven-day sample menu plan that I have included as part of the elimination diet. These recipes are all suitable for the elimination phase—and anytime. If you are cooking for guests, these taste great and you won't need to tell anyone that these comply with a special elimination diet.

BEVERAGES

CHAI LATTE

Chai tea is a delicious low-FODMAP spiced-up tea. You can enjoy hot or iced; try making a batch now and saving some for later.

MAKES 1 SERVING

1 cup water
½ cup lactose-free milk or almond milk
1 tea bag, or 2 teaspoons loose black tea
4 cardamom pods
1 cinnamon stick
One 1-inch piece peeled ginger, sliced
3 black peppercorns
½ teaspoon fennel seeds
Sugar

Heat the water and milk to a simmer in a small saucepan over medium heat; do not let boil. Add all the remaining ingredients and cook, stirring, for 2 minutes. Pour the mixture through a strainer into a mug and enjoy.

GOLDEN MILK

This beverage has powerful anti-inflammatory benefits from the turmeric, which also gives this drink its beautiful golden color.

MAKES 1 SERVING

1½ cups almond milk
1 tablespoon coconut oil
1 tablespoon pure maple syrup
1 teaspoon ground turmeric
½ teaspoon ground cinnamon, or 1 cinnamon stick
One 1-inch piece peeled ginger

Heat the almond milk to a simmer in a small saucepan over medium heat; do not let boil. Add all the remaining ingredients and cook, stirring, for about 2 minutes. Remove the ginger. Enjoy!

JUICES

INGREDIENTS YOU CAN ADD TO JUICES—MIX AND MATCH!

Beets—limit to 2 slices

Carrots

Celery—limit to ½ stalk per serving

Cucumber

Ginger

Honeydew melon

Kale

Lemon

Lime

Orange

Pineapple

Spinach

Swiss chard

Tomato, limit to ½ cup

Wash the selected ingredients and roughly chop the larger items. Cut the skin off hard items, such as lemon. Place each ingredient in a juicer and juice. I try not to be overly precise when making juices—as long as you are limiting the items that I have mentioned, you should be fine. Enjoy!

Each of the following combinations should yield approximately 1 cup.

Orange Refresher

¾ cup carrot juice (about 6 carrots)

1 orange, peeled

¼ lime, peeled

One ½-inch piece peeled ginger

Thirst Quencher

2 slices beet
½ cucumber
1 bunch kale
¼ lemon, peeled

Health Kicker

6 carrots
½ bunch kale
¼ lemon, peeled
One ½-inch piece peeled ginger

Savory Blend

½ cup tomato juice
½ cup carrot juice (about 4 carrots)
1 celery stalk
½ lemon, peeled

SMOOTHIES

Smoothies are a great quick meal that you can still enjoy on the elimination phase of the low-FODMAP diet. Some things to keep in mind are that smoothies are commonly consumed with a straw, and that drinking through a straw introduces air into your system, so skip the straw and sip. Also, because smoothies are easy to drink and delicious, we have a tendency to consume them very quickly—so be mindful and pace yourself. Finally, what is the next word you think of when you hear "smoothie"? Fruit! And fruit is certainly not something we want to avoid entirely. But the smoothie should not contain unlimited amounts of fruits, even if the fruits come from the low-FODMAP lists, we want to limit to one portion of fruit per smoothie. Each of the following recipes makes one serving.

SUITABLE FRUITS FOR SMOOTHIES—MIX AND MATCH
Avocados—limit to ⅛ per serving during elimination phase
Bananas
Blueberries
Cantaloupe
Coconut
Dragon fruit
Passion fruit
Papayas
Raspberries
Strawberries

Remember, fruits commonly used in smoothies that you should avoid during the elimination phase are:

Apples
Pears
Mangoes
Watermelon

Strawberry Almond Smoothie

½ banana, frozen
¼ cup strawberries
½ cup spinach
½ cup almond milk
2 tablespoons almond butter

Peanut Butter Banana Smoothie

½ banana, frozen
¼ cup blueberries
½ cup chopped kale
2 tablespoons peanut butter
½ cup almond milk

Creamy Nutty Smoothie

⅓ cup lactose-free yogurt
¾ cup almond milk
½ banana, frozen
2 tablespoons almond butter
¼ teaspoon ground cinnamon

BREAKFASTS

OATMEAL WITH SLICED ALMONDS AND BLUEBERRIES

You don't need to be a chef to make this hearty, traditional breakfast. This recipe yields 1 cup of cooked oats, but I like to make a larger batch (keeping the 2:1 proportion of water to oats) and store it in the refrigerator. Chilled, it forms a cakelike consistency that I can easily slice and reheat in the microwave. When I cook it in batches, I do not add the toppings until I am going to eat the oatmeal. You could also add toppings to the saucepan as you first cook the oatmeal, if you prefer. Alternatively, you can prepare the oatmeal in a rice cooker.

SERVES 2

1 cup water
½ cup steel-cut oats
3 tablespoons sliced almonds, optionally toasted
½ cup blueberries
½ banana, sliced
2 tablespoons chia seeds (optional)

Place the water in a saucepan over medium-high heat and bring to a boil. Add the oats and lower the heat to a simmer. Stirring occasionally, cook for about 15 minutes, or until the water is mostly cooked out and the oatmeal appears at the proper consistency for eating. Top with the almonds, blueberries, bananas, and chia seeds, if using.

Other low-FODMAP oatmeal toppers:
Brown sugar and pure maple syrup
Chopped walnuts and cinnamon
Minced chives and radishes
Miso paste and chopped walnuts
Olive oil and salt
Sliced banana and powdered peanut butter

FARM OMELET WITH PEPPERS AND SPINACH

Eggs are an energy-packed way to start the day, but can also be a great quick dinner. You can easily swap in other vegetables as you wish, or even throw in some Cheddar or Parmesan.

SERVES 2

Olive oil or nonstick cooking spray
½ diced bell pepper (red, yellow, or green)
½ cup spinach
4 large eggs
¼ cup lactose-free milk
Salt and freshly ground black pepper

Heat a skillet over medium-high heat, and coat lightly with olive oil or nonstick cooking spray. Cook the bell pepper and spinach for a few minutes, until the spinach is wilted and the pepper has softened.

Whisk together the eggs and milk in a bowl. Pour the eggs onto the vegetable mixture in the skillet and cook until slightly set, about 2 minutes, placing your omelet additions on the center of the eggs before the eggs have set. Fold the omelet in half and continue to cook until the eggs are fully cooked.

Other low-FODMAP omelet fillers:
Avocado
Bacon
Cheddar
Chives
Feta
Peppers
Smoked salmon
Spinach

CHIA PUDDING

This is another superquick and easy, energy-packed recipe that you can make ahead and have ready in your fridge for when you have a sweet craving! It fills you up without making you bloated. Enjoy your chia pudding plain, or add toppings—such as cacao nibs or a serving of blueberries or strawberries. You can even use homemade trail mix (page 153) or any of the oatmeal toppings on page 113.

SERVES 2

2 cups almond or coconut milk
6 tablespoons chia seeds
2 teaspoons pure maple syrup
1 teaspoon vanilla extract

Combine the milk, chia seeds, maple syrup, and vanilla in a blender. Blend for about 1 minute, or until mixed evenly. Pour into either one large jar to portion later, or into individual-size jars. Store in the refrigerator overnight, or for at least 12 hours, until settled.

FLAT STOMACH FRENCH TOAST

An elimination diet is not a deprivation diet. Enjoy this classic breakfast treat and do not feel guilty about it! You won't need to make any compromises with the maple syrup because that is a top-choice low-FODMAP sweetener.

SERVES 2

3 large eggs
½ cup lactose-free milk
½ teaspoon ground cinnamon, plus extra for topping
4 pieces suitable low-FODMAP bread (see page 178).
Nonstick cooking spray or unsalted butter, for pan
1 banana, sliced
Sliced almonds (optional)
Powdered sugar (optional)
Pure maple syrup, for serving

Mix together the eggs, milk, and cinnamon in a medium bowl or baking dish. Lay the slices of bread in the mixture to coat. Place, covered, in the refrigerator overnight for best results. Otherwise, let soak for as long as possible.

Spray a large skillet with nonstick cooking spray or grease with butter and heat over medium heat. Lay the soaked bread in the pan (you may need to work in batches) and cook each side for about 5 minutes, or until lightly browned . Top each slice of French toast with sliced banana. Sprinkle with ground cinnamon, almonds, and powdered sugar, if using, and serve with maple syrup.

CHOCOLATE CHIP BANANA BREAKFAST COOKIES

Sure, we think of cookies as a treat—but you will see that all of the ingredients in these cookies make them a good choice for any time of day, even breakfast. The flaxseeds make this is a high-fiber choice and will keep you feeling more satisfied than you ever imagined a cookie could.

MAKES 40 BITE-SIZE COOKIES

3 large, ripe bananas
2 cups rolled oats
1 cup almond butter
⅓ cup dark chocolate chips
3 tablespoons hemp seeds
¼ cup pure maple syrup
5 tablespoons flaxseeds mixed with 1 cup plus 1 tablespoon
   water (to form "flaxseed eggs")
2 teaspoons vanilla extract
1½ teaspoons ground cinnamon
Pinch of sea salt

Preheat the oven to 350°F. Line a baking sheet with parchment paper.

Place the bananas in a large bowl and mash with a fork. Add the oats, almond butter, chocolate chips, hemp seeds, maple syrup, "flaxseed eggs," vanilla, cinnamon, and salt, and mix until well combined. Form the dough into 1-inch balls and place them an inch apart on the prepared baking sheet. Flatten them with the back of a spoon.

Bake for 12 to 15 minutes, until the edges start to brown. Remove from the oven and allow to cool for a minute, then transfer to a wire rack to cool.

The cookies can be stored in an airtight container in the refrigerator for up to 1 week.

Recipe provided by Triad to Wellness LLC, www.triadtowellness.com.

MAINS

FARMHOUSE FRITTATA

Frittatas rock—breakfast, brunch, lunch, or dinner—no matter the time you can whip this up for friends and no one will know it is low-FODMAP. Enjoy with a salad, or even lactose-free yogurt. This recipe serves four—a frittata is a great thing to make now and save for later.

SERVES 4

2 tablespoons olive oil, plus more (or nonstick cooking spray) for pan
10 large eggs
Salt and freshly ground black pepper
½ cup chopped kale
½ cup chopped zucchini
½ cup chopped broccoli
¼ cup chopped cherry tomatoes
¼ cup grated Parmesan

Preheat the oven to 350°F. Oil an 8-inch round cake pan with olive oil or nonstick cooking spray.

In a bowl, mix together the eggs until well combined. Add a pinch each of salt and pepper.

Heat the 2 tablespoons of olive oil in a large skillet over medium-high heat, then add the kale and zucchini and season to taste with salt and pepper. Cook over medium heat for 5 to 7 minutes, until the vegetables are softened and begin to brown. Remove from the heat and carefully add the cooked vegetables to the egg mixture, stirring so that they are evenly distributed. (You can add other vegetables here, too, if you have them already cooked, such as roasted potatoes.) Once the vegetables are mixed in, transfer the mixture to the prepared cake pan and top evenly with the Parmesan.

Place in the oven and bake for about 20 minutes, or until a toothpick inserted into the center comes out clean.

ROASTED CHICKEN PROVENÇAL WITH RATATOUILLE

It's good to have a low-FODMAP chicken recipe on hand. Roasted chicken breasts are very versatile and you can include them in many meals as your protein. With this recipe you get the bonus of building a vegetable side dish right into the main course. You could make these separately—but you get two for one when you make this delicious combination. Serve with quinoa or basmati rice.

SERVES 2

1 tablespoon plus ½ teaspoon olive oil
Two 6-ounce skinless, boneless chicken breast halves
1 ½ cups diced eggplant
⅓ cup diced red bell pepper
½ cup diced zucchini
2 tablespoons dried oregano
¼ cup fresh tarragon, finely chopped
3 tablespoons fresh rosemary, finely chopped
½ teaspoon coriander seeds
1 tablespoon unsalted butter
1 tablespoon buckwheat flour
Salt and freshly ground black pepper

Preheat the oven to 275°F. Cover a sheet pan with foil.

Heat 1 tablespoon of the olive oil in a large skillet over high heat, then add the chicken. Cook for 1 to 2 minutes, until slightly golden, turn the chicken over, and cook for 1 to 2 minutes more. Remove the chicken from the pan, set it aside on a plate, and allow it to cool to room temperature.

Meanwhile, mix the vegetables, tarragon, rosemary, and coriander seeds together in a medium bowl and set aside.

Mix the butter and buckwheat flour together in a small bowl to create a paste and spread it evenly over the chicken. Gently pat the vegetable mixture onto the chicken, setting the remaining vegetable mixture aside. Season the chicken with salt and black pepper.

Arrange the chicken and remaining vegetable mixture on the prepared sheet pan. Brush the remaining ½ teaspoon of olive oil over the extra vegetable mixture. Place the pan in the oven and roast for 8 to 10 minutes, or until the chicken is cooked white throughout. Transfer the chicken to individual serving plates. Mix the remaining vegetables and pan juices in a bowl and spoon over the chicken.

Recipe provided by Epicured, gourmet low-FODMAP meal delivery service www.getepicured.com.

COCONUT-CRUSTED CHICKEN

This looks like fried chicken, but it is so much better for you—while still tasting great. This is one that the whole family will enjoy. You can even serve this dish with ketchup, as long as it doesn't contain high-fructose corn syrup.

SERVES 2

1½ teaspoons coconut oil
1½ teaspoons pure maple syrup
2 tablespoons coconut milk
⅓ cup finely shredded unsweetened coconut
½ cup unsweetened brown rice cereal
⅛ teaspoon sea salt
¼ teaspoon freshly ground black pepper
Two 4-ounce skinless, boneless chicken breasts, cut into strips,
  or chicken tenders

Preheat the oven to 400°F. Coat a baking sheet with the coconut oil and set aside.

Place the maple syrup and coconut milk in a medium bowl and mix well. Place the shredded coconut, brown rice cereal, salt, and pepper in a zip-top plastic bag and crush well. Dredge the chicken strips in the coconut milk mixture and place a few at a time in the bag, to coat with the coconut mixture. Transfer to the prepared baking sheet. Bake for 7 to 8 minutes per side, until the chicken is cooked through to 165°F.

Notes: You can add ¼ teaspoon of red pepper flakes or cayenne pepper for extra spiciness. You can also substitute cornflakes for the brown rice cereal.

Recipe provided by Triad to Wellness LLC, www.triadtowellness.com.

VEGETABLE STIR-FRY

This is a versatile dish; you can easily switch out these vegetables for whatever you have on hand. You can also add ground beef or chicken. For enhanced flavor, if you are going to add meat, cook the vegetables first, remove them from the pan, and cook the meat separately. Then, combine before serving. Enjoy the stir-fry on top of brown rice, quinoa, or rice noodles.

SERVES 2

1 tablespoon olive oil or other neutral oil
½ cup chopped eggplant
½ cup sliced bell peppers
2 carrots, peeled and julienned
½ cup chopped broccoli
½ cup chopped kale
4 ounces firm tofu, or 2 large eggs
2 scallions (green part only), chopped in quarter-inch pieces
2 tablespoons Miso Dressing (page 165) or Teriyaki Sauce (page 168)

Heat the oil in a large skillet over medium-high heat. Add the eggplant, peppers, and carrots and cook for about 5 minutes, or until slightly softened. Add the broccoli, kale, tofu, and scallions and continue to cook. If using eggs, stir to scramble. After another 3 to 4 minutes, stir in the miso dressing or teriyaki sauce and cook for another 3 to 4 minutes.

SESAME-CRUSTED TUNA

An easy-to-make recipe for any night of the week. This is a go-to in my home for a protein-packed dinner that hits the spot for both sweet and salty tastes. The Asian-influenced marinade packs flavor, and will leave you feeling bloat-free. Serve with green beans.

SERVES 2

2 tablespoons soy sauce or gluten-free tamari
2 tablespoons rice vinegar
1 teaspoon grated peeled ginger
Two 6-ounce tuna fillets
3 tablespoons sesame seeds (white, black, or combination)

Combine the soy sauce, rice vinegar, and ginger in a bowl to create a marinade, and let the tuna soak in this marinade for at least 1 hour. (You may find that it is convenient to do this in a zip-top plastic bag.)

Preheat the oven to 350°F. Line a baking sheet with foil.

Spread out the sesame seeds on a plate and lay down the tuna so that the sesame seeds coat one side of the fish in an even layer. You can coat the entire fillet, if desired. Place the tuna, seed side up, on the prepared baking sheet. Bake for 15 minutes, check the internal temperature (a safe internal temperature for cooked tuna is 125°F), and bake for 5 more minutes, if necessary.

NIÇOISE SALAD

A classic French salad made the low-FODMAP way! All it takes is a few tweaks to make your favorite foods fit into your low-FODMAP life. You won't even notice the difference.

SERVES 2

For the salad:
2 cups mixed lettuce
One 5-ounce can oil-packed tuna
2 to 3 hard-boiled eggs
½ cup green beans, washed and sliced
10 olives
1 tablespoon capers

For the vinaigrette:
2 teaspoons cider vinegar
2 teaspoons Dijon mustard
2 tablespoons olive oil
2 teaspoons chives, washed and minced
Salt and freshly ground black pepper

Combine the salad ingredients in a bowl.

To prepare the vinaigrette, whisk together the vinegar and mustard and slowly whisk in the olive oil until emulsified. Whisk in the chives and season with salt and pepper to taste. Drizzle over the salad before serving.

QUINOA SALAD

If you invite me over for a potluck, there is a good chance this is what I am bringing with me. And for good reason: everyone loves it. It's gluten- and dairy-free and full of complex flavor. This one is sure to impress your family and friends.

SERVES 2

1 cup water
½ cup uncooked quinoa, rinsed
1 tablespoon olive oil
1 teaspoon cider vinegar
1 teaspoon pure maple syrup
¼ teaspoon ground cinnamon
¼ cup sliced almonds
1 tablespoon dried cranberries
1 scallion (green part only), chopped in quarter-inch pieces

Bring the water to a boil in a medium saucepan over medium-high heat. Add the quinoa and lower the heat to a simmer. Cook until the water is cooked out and the quinoa looks to have little "halo" formed on it. Remove from the heat and transfer the quinoa to a serving bowl.

In a small bowl, whisk together the olive oil, vinegar, maple syrup, and cinnamon to make a dressing.

Toast the almonds in a dry skillet over medium-high heat for about 1 minute, or until just fragrant and slightly toasted. Be careful not to overtoast!

Toss the toasted almonds, dried cranberries, and scallion into the quinoa to combine. Pour the dressing over the quinoa and toss to mix evenly.

MORE SALAD IDEAS

There are endless combinations of salads that you can enjoy during the elimination phase of the diet. You can eat salads as you typically would; just remove any high-FODMAP ingredients. If you are looking for some fresh ideas, here are a few salads you can try:

Garden salad: Mix romaine lettuce, sliced tomato, sliced carrot, Cheddar, and a hard-boiled egg. Top with balsamic vinaigrette.

Greek salad: Mix chopped cucumber, olives, sliced tomato, dill, and feta. Top with olive oil and lemon juice. Season to taste with salt and freshly ground black pepper.

Corn and squash salad: Heat a little olive oil in a skillet, add the corn from ½ cob plus sliced summer squash, and cook for 3 to 4 minutes. Top with some chopped fresh basil, and season to taste with salt and freshly ground black pepper.

Green bean salad: Cut green beans into 1-inch pieces and blanch in boiling water. Combine with sliced radishes, cucumber, and hard-boiled eggs. Top with olive oil and season to taste with salt and freshly ground black pepper.

Tuna salad: Mix one 5-ounce can of tuna with 1 tablespoon of mayonnaise and 2 teaspoons of lemon juice. Season to taste with salt and freshly ground black pepper. You can add ¼ stalk of celery sliced in ⅛-inch pieces per serving, for some crunch.

VEGETABLES

SPINACH SAUTÉED WITH PINE NUTS

A versatile side dish that pairs well with just about any entrée. You can use it to serve as a bed for protein, or enjoy as a snack with eggs.

SERVES 2

1 tablespoon pine nuts
1 tablespoon olive oil or garlic-infused oil (for homemade, see page 154)
2 cups spinach, washed
2 teaspoons fresh lemon juice
Shaved Parmesan to garnish

Place the pine nuts in a dry skillet over medium heat and toast for about 2 minutes, or until just browning and becoming fragrant. Remove the pine nuts from the skillet and set aside. Add the olive oil to the skillet and heat. Add the spinach and lemon juice to the skillet and cook for about 5 minutes, until just wilted. Toss with the toasted pine nuts and top with shaved Parmesan.

ROASTED SPICED CARROTS

The sweet taste of carrots is even better when they are roasted. You can enjoy this as a side dish or on top of rice or quinoa.

SERVES 2

½ pound carrots
1 tablespoon coconut oil
½ teaspoon garam masala or salt and pepper

Preheat the oven to 425°F. Line a baking sheet with tin foil.

Wash and peel carrots, and cut up so that all the pieces are about the same size. I typically cut the pieces into carrot sticks. Coat the carrots with the coconut oil—either heat and melt the coconut oil in advance, or get your hands dirty spreading it around. Sprinkle with garam masala or salt and pepper. Roast in the oven for 20 minutes and then check; the carrots are finished when there is slight browning on edges.

SAUTÉED BOK CHOY

Bok choy has grown from being an exotic and unknown vegetable to becoming one of my favorites—it has a great flavor, and it's easy to cook. It is packed with vitamins, and it won't upset your gut. Win-win-win!

SERVES 2

1 tablespoon garlic-infused oil (for homemade, see page 154)
2 teaspoons grated peeled ginger
2 cups chopped bok choy
1 tablespoon soy sauce
Salt and freshly ground black pepper

Heat the garlic-infused oil in a skillet over medium-high heat. Add the ginger to the oil and cook for 1 minute or so, try not to let it burn. Add the bok choy and soy sauce and cook for about 5 minutes, or until just wilted. Season to taste with salt and pepper.

Note: Soy sauce is not gluten-free, but in small quantities it is suitable for the elimination phase of the low-FODMAP diet.

ROSEMARY ROASTED POTATOES

Who doesn't love roasted potatoes? Roast these up in advance and serve as a side dish for days. You can serve with meat or even with eggs at breakfast.

SERVES 2

½ pound small new potatoes
1 to 2 tablespoons olive oil or garlic-infused oil (for homemade, see page 154)
½ teaspoon salt
¼ teaspoon freshly ground black pepper
1 tablespoon fresh rosemary, or 1 teaspoon dried

Preheat the oven to 425°F. Line a baking sheet with foil.

Slice the potatoes into equal-size pieces about the size of a Ping-Pong ball, or smaller, and place in a single layer on the prepared pan. Pour the oil over the potatoes and spread as evenly as possible. Sprinkle with the salt, pepper, and rosemary. Roast in the oven for about 30 minutes, checking to ensure that the potatoes are browning evenly.

> **Fresh or Dried Herbs?**
> You can use either, but because dried herbs are more potent you can use less—about 1 teaspoon of dried herbs is the flavor equivalent of 1 tablespoon of fresh herbs.

GREEN BEANS WITH ALMONDS

An excellent side dish to go with just about any meal. You might even get fancy and try it as a snack.

SERVES 2

2 tablespoons sliced almonds
1 tablespoon sesame seeds
1 tablespoon sesame oil, preferably toasted
1 tablespoon grapeseed or other neutral oil
12 ounces green beans, trimmed

Place the almonds in a dry skillet over medium heat and toast for 1 to 2 minutes, until beginning to get fragrant, but not burning. Remove from the heat and transfer to a bowl. Repeat the process with the sesame seeds, placing them in the same bowl as the toasted almonds. (You want to toast the almonds and sesame seeds separately because they may need to toast for different times and it would be difficult to remove only one or the other if the pan is shared.)

Heat the sesame oil and grapeseed oil in a large skillet over medium heat and add the green beans. Lower the heat to medium-low and cook for 5 to 7 minutes, watching to make sure there is no burning. The green beans should start to blister. Remove the green beans from the heat and stir in the toasted almonds and sesame seeds.

ROASTED EGGPLANT
WITH TAHINI

This is a favorite in my household. I think eggplants have the most incredible and complex flavor—you won't miss garlic or onions for a second.

SERVES 2

1 tablespoon olive oil, plus 1 tablespoon (or nonstick cooking spray) for pan
1 large eggplant
½ teaspoon salt
¼ teaspoon freshly ground black pepper
2 tablespoons tahini (sesame seed butter)

Preheat the oven to 375°F. Line a baking sheet with foil, and use about 1 tablespoon of olive oil or nonstick cooking spray to coat the foil.

Slice the eggplant into ½-inch-thick rounds, and lay out in a single layer on the prepared baking sheet (you may need to cook in batches or use more than one baking sheet). Coat the eggplant lightly with the tablespoon of olive oil (use a brush to spread evenly; otherwise, use your fingers). Sprinkle with the salt and pepper. Roast for about 20 minutes, checking to see that the eggplant slices are cooking evenly. They are finished when slightly translucent and browned.

Serve with tahini on top.

CINNAMON SWEET POTATOES

Sweet potato makes an excellent side dish, especially with a pinch of cinnamon to enhance its flavor. This one is super simple, but food doesn't need to be complicated to taste good and make you feel great.

MAKES 2 SERVINGS

1 tablespoon olive oil, plus more for pan
1 large sweet potato
½ teaspoon ground cinnamon

Preheat the oven to 425°F. Line a baking sheet with foil and lightly oil the foil to prevent sticking.

Wash, peel, and chop the sweet potato into ½-inch cubes. Toss the potatoes in a bowl with the olive oil to coat evenly. Spread out the potato cubes in one layer on the prepared baking sheet. Sprinkle with the cinnamon. Roast for 30 minutes and then check: When the potato cubes are slightly browned and you are able to pierce one easily with a fork, they are finished.

ZUCCHINI NOODLES

Sure, you can eat gluten-free pasta, but zucchini noodles are way cooler. They are packed with vitamins and easily digested fiber, not to mention delicious and fun to make.

SERVES 2

1 medium zucchini

Cut the ends off the zucchini and use a spiralizer to make noodles. Once finished, gather up the zucchini noodles and blanch for 1 minute in boiling water. Remove the noodles from the water immediately and let dry on a paper towel. Serve with suitable tomato sauce or Basil Pesto (page 167).

STAPLES

HOMEMADE TRAIL MIX

You can put this mix into a bag to take on the go; it is a perfect airplane or car snack. Or you can enjoy it as a topping on yogurt—either lactose-free yogurt, almond milk yogurt, or coconut yogurt— or as a topping for your chia pudding.

IDEAS TO INCLUDE IN YOUR TRAIL MIX—MIX AND MATCH:

Almonds

Coconut flakes (do not exceed ¼ cup per portion)

Cranberries, dried (up to 1 tablespoon per portion; sweetened with sugar—check the ingredient list because some brands are sweetened with apple juice or artificial sweeteners)

Dark chocolate chips (do not exceed 1 ounce per portion)

Hazelnuts

Macadamia nuts

Pecans

Sunflower seeds (do not exceed ¼ cup per portion)

Walnuts

This one is really easy. Combine and enjoy—you can portion it out into small zip-top bags to take with you on the go.

GARLIC-INFUSED OIL

3 garlic cloves
4 tablespoons olive oil

Combine the garlic and olive oil in a small skillet over medium-low heat. Let the flavors of the garlic infuse into the oil over a period of 3 to 4 minutes, until fragrant. Try not to let the garlic burn. Remove from the heat and let cool, then remove and discard the garlic and use the oil in your recipe.

Note: Do not store this home-infused garlic for later use. If you want garlic oil on hand for recipes, you can purchase garlic-infused oil at a grocery store.

MEDITERRANEAN EGGPLANT DIP

Eggplant has the most complex flavors, and while store-bought varieties of eggplant-based dips contain garlic, if you make it yourself you will find that you are not missing garlic at all. Enjoy this dip with cut-up carrots or cucumbers.

MAKES 4 SERVINGS

1 large eggplant
2 tablespoons olive oil
3 tablespoons tahini (sesame seed butter)
1 tablespoon fresh lemon juice
1 tablespoon chopped fresh parsley
Salt and freshly ground black pepper

Preheat the oven to 450°F. Line a baking dish with foil.

Cut the eggplant in half, place in the prepared baking dish, coat with olive oil, and roast in the oven for about 15 minutes, or until the center softens so that there is no tension when you pierce with a fork. Remove from the oven and let cool.

Remove the inner part of the eggplant and place in a medium bowl. You can discard the eggplant skins. Combine the eggplant with the tahini, lemon juice, and parsley. Season to taste with salt and pepper.

HOMEMADE HUMMUS

This recipe is a favorite: hummus is a tasty popular snack, but I have yet to find one on the store shelves that does not contain onion or garlic. Luckily it is very easy to make yourself with a blender. Share with friends, or enjoy it yourself over a few days. You can adjust the portion size as needed. Because chickpeas should only be enjoyed in smaller quantities during the elimination phase of this diet, be sure to place the hummus you are eating in a preportioned serving on your plate so you don't overindulge, or make one serving at a time.

MAKES 4 SERVINGS

1 cup canned chickpeas, drained and rinsed with water
¼ cup tahini (sesame seed butter)
¼ cup olive oil
¼ cup fresh lemon juice
½ teaspoon salt
Paprika (optional)

Combine all the ingredients in a blender. Dust with paprika, if using, and enjoy with cut-up carrots, cucumbers, peppers, or suitable crackers (see page 180 for suggested brands).

STRAWBERRY CHIA JAM

When I learned that you could make jam from chia seeds, I thought it was just about the coolest thing I had ever heard. But it makes sense: those little seeds turn to a gelatinous gel when combined with liquid. This recipe is excellent, fun for the whole family, and so much easier than making jam in a more traditional way. Chia seeds are a favorite source of low-FODMAP fiber, and this is definitely a unique way to include them in your diet.

MAKES 1 CUP OF JAM

2 cups hulled and chopped strawberries
1 teaspoon vanilla extract
1 to 2 teaspoons balsamic vinegar
1 tablespoon pure maple syrup
3 tablespoons chia seeds

Place the strawberries, vanilla, balsamic vinegar, and maple syrup in a saucepan. Bring to a gentle boil over medium heat, then lower the heat to a simmer and cook for 10 minutes, during which time the fruit will become syrupy and thicker. Continue to cook, stirring and mashing the fruit, until it reaches your desired consistency. Once the mixture is thickened, remove the saucepan from the heat. Add the chia seeds and stir thoroughly.

For a smoother jam you can blend the mixture in a blender until you reach the desired consistency, or use an immersion blender directly in the saucepan. Let the jam sit for at least 5 minutes until it sets. Refrigerating the jam for 1 hour or overnight will produce a thicker jam. Once the jam has cooled to room temperature, transfer the mixture to a jar or other lidded glass container and let it set for 5 minutes. Taste and adjust the sweetness, if necessary.

Store, tightly covered, in the refrigerator for up to 2 weeks.

Recipe provided by Triad to Wellness LLC, www.triadtowellness.com.

THE GIRL WHO LOVED TOO MUCH FRUIT

Rebecca, age 24, was an athlete who used to love running but was now held back, weighed down by her distended and uncomfortable digestive issues. She had a number of food allergies as well—including peanuts and soy—that were not related to her abdominal issues but made her diet more limited. She had already been to the doctor to rule out other diagnoses and it was determined that she had IBS. At first she would get occasional stomachaches, but now she was also feeling bloating and distended and it was getting in the way of what she loved doing. She opted to start with a dietary treatment, and my first step was looking over her three-day diet record so that I could assess it for potential triggers. What I found is not uncommon: Everything she ate was "healthy" but she still felt terrible.

It seemed to me that to compensate for her other food allergies, she was overloading on fruit. Breakfast was eggs, an apple, dried figs, and cherries. Lunch was accompanied by melon, pineapple, and grapes. Dessert was a bowl of blueberries and blackberries. Other than the fruit, she was also eating lean meats, Greek yogurt, and salads. Rebecca's sister was a nutritionist—and as a result of her passion for nutrition, the whole family had incredibly "healthy" diets. I made one big suggestion for the first week—to limit her fruit intake to one serving per meal of low-FODMAP fruits. I didn't even touch on the other items in her diet, such as the Greek yogurt, at this point. I was reading for signs in her reaction, and as someone who was health-conscious, she was pretty stunned that a registered dietitian was telling her to eat *less* fruit. Although she obliged and agreed to try this, I felt I would be pushing it to try to suggest other dramatic changes to foods she viewed as healthy.

Two weeks later she came into my office, wearing running clothes—she was back to feeling like herself and back to running. It was a dramatic result—and she still ate fruit; she just changed what types and how much of it she was having. Although limiting the fruit was a great start, we did take a look at other triggers that were present in Rebecca's diet. We ended up going through and hand picking any potential issues—in her case, she loved yogurt. I suggested a lactose-free yogurt that she was able to swap in. Two years later, she continues to feel great on the low-FODMAP diet, limiting her fruit intake as well as her lactose intake.

This year, I was at a party and started chatting with another nutritionist. I told her about my specialty in helping people with digestive issues to find relief with the low-FODMAP diet. She told me the story of her sister who met with a dietitian who changed her life by putting her on that diet—it was exciting for both of us when we realized that her sister was Rebecca!

FRUIT SALAD

On the elimination diet, you do not want to exceed one serving of fruit per meal or snack. But that does not mean you should avoid fruit, and you still have a wide variety of options to enjoy. The following is a list of serving sizes for suitable fruits. To make a fruit salad, you can combine different fruits from this list—as long as they add up to one total serving of fruit. Following the list, I have provided some examples as to what a serving of fruit salad would look like.

ONE SERVING OF FRUIT IS:

Banana: 1 medium

Blueberries: 20

Cantaloupe: ½ cup

Clementine: 1 medium

Coconut: ½ cup

Dragon fruit: 1 medium

Grapes: 1 cup

Guava: 1 medium

Honeydew melon: ½ cup

Kiwis: 2 small peeled

Kumquats: 4

Orange: 1 medium

Passion fruit: 1 whole (pulp)

Papaya: 1 cup, chopped

Pineapple: 1 cup, chopped

Pomegranate: ¼ cup seeds, or ½ small

Prickly pear: 1 medium

Raspberries: 10

Rhubarb: 1 cup, chopped

Star fruit: 1 medium

Strawberries: 10

ONE SERVING OF A LOW-FODMAP FRUIT SALAD MIGHT BE:

Strawberries: 5

Melon: ¼ cup

Grapes: ⅓ cup

OR

Kiwi: 1 small

Pineapple: ⅓ cup

Blueberries: 10

BASIC VINAIGRETTE

The general rule in making salad dressing is
to use a ratio of three parts oil to one part acid
(lemon juice or vinegar). Gradually whisk in the
oil to incorporate. Add salt and freshly ground
black pepper to taste. Olive oil works nicely here.
You can experiment with different oils. You can
also try different vinegars (apple cider vinegar,
rice vinegar, balsamic vinegar). Remember
to limit balsamic vinegar to no more than
1 tablespoon per serving.

Optional add-ins: Minced fresh herbs, such as basil, rosemary,
tarragon, or thyme, or dried herbs

For a garlic vinaigrette: Replace part of the oil with garlic-
infused oil (for homemade, see page 154).

> **Salad Dressings**
> Many salad dressings on grocery store shelves contain high-
> FODMAP ingredients, such as onion or garlic, so this is one thing
> you may want to master for yourself.

BALSAMIC VINAIGRETTE

This recipe yields enough dressing for one salad. Feel free to make as much as you need.

2 teaspoons balsamic vinegar
1 teaspoon Dijon mustard
2 tablespoons olive oil

Place the balsamic vinegar and mustard in a small bowl and slowly pour in the olive oil, whisking to incorporate.

CARROT GINGER DRESSING

This is a low-FODMAP version of the sweet dressing that is served in Japanese restaurants. To increase the consistency of this dressing, you can puree a carrot rather than using carrot juice. This recipe yields enough dressing for a stir-fry or salad, you can always make extra.

1 tablespoon rice vinegar
1 tablespoon carrot juice, or 1 carrot, pureed
1 teaspoon grated peeled ginger
½ teaspoon soy sauce
½ teaspoon sesame oil
¼ teaspoon sugar
Salt and freshly ground black pepper

Place all the ingredients, except the salt and pepper, in a small bowl and stir to combine. Season to taste with salt and pepper.

MISO DRESSING

Miso provides a savory flavor that will boost any meal. One way to incorporate this probiotic-rich, low-FODMAP ingredient is in a dressing. You can enjoy this on a salad, or on rice, quinoa, noodles, or sautéed kale as a sauce. You can also use this in a stir-fry to add some Asian-inspired flavor. This recipe yields enough dressing for a stir-fry or salad; feel free to make extra.

1 tablespoon unseasoned rice vinegar
1 tablespoon white miso
2 teaspoons grated peeled ginger
½ teaspoon sugar
1 tablespoon soy sauce
1 teaspoon sesame oil

Place all the ingredients in a small bowl and stir to combine.

BASIL PESTO

Pesto is a great way to add flavor and nutrients to your food. If you buy pesto in a store, it is pretty much guaranteed to contain garlic as one of the main ingredients. It is possible to achieve excellent taste without compromising how you feel at the end of the meal. This basil pesto delivers exceptional taste without FODMAPs. Enjoy with zucchini noodles, on gluten-free pasta, with vegetables or chicken dishes. This recipe yields ¾ cup of pesto, which is about eight portions if you use 2 tablespoons per portion. You can freeze extra in ice cube trays for later use.

2½ cups fresh basil leaves (about 2 bunches)
½ bunch chives
2 tablespoons garlic-infused olive oil (for homemade, see
   page 154)
2 tablespoons olive oil
3 tablespoons grated Parmesan
3 tablespoons pine nuts
Salt

Have ready a bowl of ice water. Bring a large quart of salted water to a boil. Blanch the basil and chives in the water for 10 to 15 seconds, then remove them and place in the bowl of ice water. Once the basil and chives are chilled, remove them from the water and squeeze out any excess water. Place the basil, chives, and remaining ingredients in a blender. Blend on medium-high speed until the sauce is smooth and thick. Season to taste with salt.

Recipe provided by Epicured, gourmet low-FODMAP meal delivery service www.getEpicured.com.

TERIYAKI SAUCE

Teriyaki is one of my favorite flavors, but unfortunately it is also one of the hardest things to make low-FODMAP because so much of the flavor comes from the addition of garlic. Luckily cookbook author and nutrition PhD Seung Hee Lee-Kwan is one of my closest friends, and she is an expert in Asian flavors. She helped me develop this recipe.

MAKES 1 CUP

1 cup light brown sugar
1 cup soy sauce
1 cup water
1 tablespoon white miso
1 tablespoon sliced ginger
5 scallions

Bring the brown sugar, soy sauce, water, and miso to a boil in a medium saucepan over medium heat, then add the ginger and scallions. Reduce to about half of the amount you started with. Remove from the heat, remove the ginger and scallions with a spoon or strainer, let cool, and use immediately or store in an airtight container in the refrigerator.

SPICE BLENDS

To make chili powder and other spice blends, mix all the ingredients well in a small bowl. Store in an airtight container. Enjoy as needed!

Asafoetida: Although on its own it does not have a great taste, this spice actually mimics the taste of onion and garlic in dishes, and so is useful as a substitute. If you have celiac disease or during the elimination diet, be sure to check the label, as some brands include wheat starch in the ingredient list.

Chili powder: Most store-bought brands contain onion or garlic, but you can easily make your own blend at home (see recipe below) and store it for use on your spice rack.

Curry powder: Buy or make at home (see recipe below). If purchasing, check labels to make sure it does not contain onion or garlic. Simply Organic brand makes a low-FODMAP elimination diet–suitable curry powder.

Garam masala: This spice blend includes black pepper, cardamom, cinnamon, coriander, and cumin. It is excellent on roasted root vegetables and in curry dishes. Most store-bought brands are low-FODMAP.

Low-FODMAP Chili Powder

2 teaspoons ground cumin

1 teaspoon paprika

¼ teaspoon cayenne pepper

1 teaspoon dried oregano

Low-FODMAP Curry Powder

4 teaspoons ground coriander

2 teaspoons ground turmeric

2 teaspoons dry mustard

2 teaspoons ground ginger

1 teaspoons cayenne powder

1 teaspspoon ground cumin

½ teaspoon ground cardamom

Appendix A:
SYMPTOM WORKSHEET

Use the following worksheet to track your symptoms during your low-FODMAP journey and monitor changes that occur from the diet.

Fill in each column using a scale of 0 to 5

0 = never experience

1 = once a month

2 = once a week

3 = three or four days per week

4 = five or six days per week

5 = every day

Definitions to keep in mind as you fill out the assessment:

Bloating: Bloating is a feeling of fullness and tightness that may or may not also have distention. In other words, you can feel bloated without looking distended.

Distention: This means that your small intestine is swollen or enlarged from internal pressure. In other words, it means that your abdomen is visibly sticking out.

SYMPTOM	FREQUENCY BEFORE LOW-FODMAP DIET	ELIMINATION PHASE
Indigestion		
Excessive gas		
Burping		
Bloating		
Abdominal distention		
Diarrhea		
Constipation		
Abdominal pain		
Exhaustion		
Irritability		
Headaches		
TOTAL		

SYMPTOM WORKSHEET: SIMPLE PLAN

Use the following worksheet to track your symptoms during the low-FODMAP simple method diet (described on page 63).

Fill in each column using a scale of 0 to 5

0 = never experience

1 = once a month

2 = once a week

3 = three or four days per week

4 = five or six days per week

5 = every day

SYMPTOM	FREQUENCY BEFORE	WEEK 1: NO LACTOSE	WEEK 2: NO EXCESS FRUCTOSE	WEEK 3: NO FRUCTANS	WEEK 4: NO GOS	WEEK 5: NO POLYOLS
Indigestion						
Excessive gas						
Burping						
Bloating						
Abdominal distention						
Diarrhea						
Constipation						
Abdominal pain						
Exhaustion						
Irritability						
Headaches						
TOTAL						

Appendix B:
TRACKING THE TESTING PHASE

You can use this chart to keep track of the results of your testing of different FODMAP categories. You will use this information to create your own personalized diet.

	TEST DAY 1 ½ PORTION	TEST DAY 2 FULL PORTION
1. Polyols: Sorbitol		
1A. Polyols: Mannitol		
2. Lactose		
3. Fructose		
4A. Fructans: Garlic		
4B. Fructans: Onion		
4C. Fructans: Wheat		
5. GOS		

Appendix C:
PORTION SIZES FOR
THE ELIMINATION DIET

Here, portion sizes are listed food by food. Note: A portion is not the same as a serving size. You can have more than one portion of foods that are not italicizedeach day. During the elimination phase, do not exceed the *italicized* portion size—the largest permitted amount of that food—for that *entire* day.

Fruits: avocado (⅛ *whole*), banana (1 medium), blueberries (20), cantaloupe (½ cup), clementine (1 medium), coconut (½ *cup*), dragon fruit (1 medium), grapes (1 cup), guava (1 medium), honeydew melon (½ cup), kiwi (2 small, peeled), kumquats (4 per portion), lemon juice (1 teaspoon), lime juice (1 teaspoon), orange (1 medium), passion fruit (1 whole pulp), papaya (1 cup chopped), pineapple (1 cup chopped), plantain (1 medium), pomegranate (*¼ cup seeds, or ½ small*), prickly pear (1 medium), raspberries (10), rhubarb (1 cup chopped), star fruit (1 medium), strawberries (10)

Dried fruits: banana chips (10 chips), coconut, shredded (*¼ cup*), cranberries (*1 tablespoon*), currants (*1 tablespoon*), raisins (*1 tablespoon*)

Vegetables: alfalfa (½ cup), bean sprouts (½ cup), beets (2 slices), bell pepper (½ cup), bok choy (1 cup), broccoli (½ cup), Brussels sprouts (2, avoid servings of 6 or more), butternut squash (*¼ cup diced*), cabbage (½ *cup*), carrot (1 medium), celery (*¼ medium* *stalk*), celery root (½ whole), cherry tomato (4 whole), chile pepper (4 inches long), chives (1 tablespoon), collard greens (1 cup), corn (½ *cob*), cucumber (½ cup), edamame (1 cup), eggplant (½ cup), endive (4 leaves), fennel bulb/leaves (½ cup), ginger (1 teaspoon fresh), green beans (12 beans), kabocha squash (½ cup diced), kale (1 cup chopped), leek (leaves only, ½ cup), lettuce (butter, iceberg, radicchio, arugula) (1 cup), okra (6 pods), olives (15 small), parsnip (½ cup), pumpkin (¼ *cup canned*), nori seaweed (2 sheets), radishes (2), scallions (green tops only, 1 bunch), snow peas (*5 pods*), spaghetti squash (1 cup), spinach (1 cup), summer squash (2 whole), sun-dried tomatoes (*2 pieces*), sweet potato (½ *cup*), Swiss chard (1 cup chopped), tomato (1 small), tomato (½ cup canned), turnip (1 cup diced), water chestnuts (½ cup sliced), white potato (1 medium), zucchini (½ cup chopped), zucchini (½ cup)

Dairy: almond milk (1 cup), Cheddar (2 slices), coconut milk (½ *cup*), Colby (2 slices), cottage cheese (4 tablespoons), feta (½ cup crumbled), goat cheese (½ cup, crumbled), goat's milk yogurt (6 ounces), Haloumi (*2 slices*), Havarti (2 slices), hemp milk (1 cup), lactose-free milk (1 cup), lactose-free yogurt (6 ounce), pecorino (½ cup grated), rice milk (¾ cup), soy milk (1 cup, only if made with soy protein), Swiss (2 slices), whipped cream (½ cup)

Grains: amaranth (¼ *cup*), cornflakes (½ cup), oatmeal (½ cup cooked), quinoa (1 cup cooked), rice (1 cup cooked)

Proteins: beef (1 small fillet), chicken (1 small fillet), chickpeas (¼ *cup, canned and drained*), eggs (2 large), firm tofu (⅔ cup), fish (100 g cooked), lamb (1 small fillet), lentils (½ *cup, canned and drained*), pork (1 small fillet), salmon (1 small fillet), sardines (110 g), shrimp (10 whole), tuna (185 g)

Nuts and seeds: almonds (*10 nuts*), Brazil nuts (10 nuts), chestnuts (10 nuts), chia seeds (2 tablespoons), hazelnuts (*10 nuts*), macadamia nuts (20 nuts), peanuts (32 nuts), pecans (10 pecan halves), pine nuts (1 tablespoon), pumpkin seeds (2 tablespoons), sunflower seeds (2 tablespoons), walnuts (10 nut halves)

Condiments: Asian fish sauce (1 tablespoon), balsamic vinegar (*1 tablespoon*), barbecue sauce (2 tablespoons; check ingredients), capers (1 tablespoon), cider vinegar (2 tablespoons), Dijon mustard (1 tablespoon), ketchup (*1 sachet; check for high-fructose corn syrup*), marmalade (2 tablespoons), mayonnaise (2 tablespoons), peanut butter (2 tablespoons), rice vinegar (2 tablespoons), strawberry jam (2 tablespoons), soy sauce (2 tablespoons), wasabi (1 teaspoon)

Fats and oils: avocado oil (1 tablespoon), butter (1 tablespoon), canola oil (1 tablespoon), coconut oil (1 tablespoon), olive oil (1 tablespoon), peanut oil (1 tablespoon), sesame oil (1 tablespoon), sunflower oil (1 tablespoon), vegetable oil (1 tablespoon)

Sweeteners: brown sugar (1 tablespoon), confectioners' sugar (1 tablespoon), dark chocolate (5 squares), granulated sugar (1 tablespoon), palm sugar (1 tablespoon), pure maple syrup (2 tablespoons), raw sugar (1 tablespoon), stevia (2 sachets; check ingredients), vanilla extract (1 tablespoon)

Herbs, fresh: basil (1 cup), cilantro (1 cup), lemongrass (4-inch stalk), parsley (1 cup), rosemary (½ cup), tarragon (1 cup), thyme (1 cup)

Spices: allspice (1 teaspoon ground), black pepper (1 teaspoon freshly ground), cardamom (1 teaspoon ground), chipotle chile powder (1 teaspoon; store-bought chili powder contains garlic; for homemade, see page 169), Chinese five-spice powder (1 teaspoon), cinnamon (1 teaspoon ground), cloves (1 teaspoon ground), coriander seeds (1 teaspoon), cumin (1 teaspoon ground), curry powder (1 teaspoon), fennel seeds (1 teaspoon), fenugreek seeds (2 tablespoons), garam masala (1 teaspoon), mustard seeds (1 teaspoon), nutmeg (1 teaspoon), paprika (1 teaspoon), saffron (1 packet), star anise (2 cloves), turmeric (1 teaspoon ground)

Appendix D:
LOW-FODMAP BRAND-NAME GROCERIES

These products have been checked to be low-FODMAP as of this writing. Once you have personalized your low-FODMAP diet, expand your selections to additional suitable products according to your needs, checking their labels very carefully for FODMAP ingredients.

BREADS
Food for Life (brown rice tortillas, multiseed English muffins)
Udi's (gluten-free white sandwich bread, whole-grain bagels, pizza crust)

CEREALS
Arrowhead Mills Puffed Rice
Bob's Red Mill (Gluten-Free Oatmeal, Mighty Tasty Hot Cereal)
Cheerios
EnviroKidz (Gorilla Munch, Peanut Butter Panda Puffs)

CONDIMENTS

FODY Foods Marinara Sauce

FODY Foods Salsa

Maille Dijon mustard

Rao's Sensitive Formula Tomato Sauce

Simply Organic curry powder

DAIRY

Green Valley Organics (lactose-free yogurt, kefir, cream cheese, sour cream)

Lifeway kefir (plain)

Lactaid milk

Organic Valley lactose-free milk

FLOURS AND BAKING MIXES

Bisquick Gluten-Free Pancake and Baking Mix

King Arthur GF Multi-Purpose Flour

Namaste Foods (waffle and pancake, brownie, and muffin mixes)

NONDAIRY BEVERAGES

8th Continent soy milk (original, light, or fat-free; other brands of soy milk are not suitable for the elimination phase)

Rice Dream (original or vanilla)

Silk almond milk

So Delicious Coconut Milk Beverage (unsweetened or vanilla)

PASTA

Ancient Harvest quinoa pastas

Barilla gluten-free pastas

Ka-Me rice sticks

Ronzoni gluten-free pastas

SNACKS

Blue Diamond Almond Nut Thins

GoMacro MacroBar (Protein Replenishment)

Ka-Me rice crackers

KIND granola bars

Lay's potato chips (sea salt)

Lundberg rice chips (sea salt)

Mary's Gone Crackers (original)

Nicer Foods Be Nice Bars

Rice cakes

Snyder's of Hanover gluten-free pretzels

Tortilla chips

SWEET TREATS

Ciao Bella (lemon, blood orange sorbet, raspberry)

Justin's Dark Chocolate Peanut Butter Cups

Lactaid vanilla ice cream

Lifeway frozen kefir

Outshine frozen fruit bars (excluding coconut, mango, peach)

Tate's Gluten-Free Chocolate Chip Cookies

RESOURCES

DANIELLE CAPALINO, MSPH, RD

www.daniellecapalino.com

My website and blog provide information about the low-FODMAP diet. You will find articles and additional recipes and resources on health and wellness.

EPICURED

https://www.getepicured.com

Epicured is New York City's first FODMAP meal delivery service. The meals are delicious and RD-approved.

FODY FOODS

https://fodyfoods.com

The founder and former CEO of Glutino has launched America's first low-FODMAP food company. They sell the foods that are hardest to find when following the low-FODMAP diet, like sauces and salsas.

GASTROGIRL

www.gastrogirl.com

Gastrogirl is a telehealth platform for patients with digestive health concerns to seek information and coaching from qualified registered dietitians.

KATE SCARLATA

www.katescarlata.com

Kate is one of the leaders in the low-FODMAP field. She has numerous resources available on her website and blog, including a list of FODMAP practitioners by state.

MONASH UNIVERSITY

http://www.med.monash.edu/cecs/gastro/fodmap/
http://fodmapmonash.blogspot.com
App: http://www.med.monash.edu/cecs/gastro/fodmap/iphone-app.html
The researchers at Monash University have pioneered the field of FOD-MAPs. They provide information for the general population via their website, blog, app, and books. If you question whether a particular food fits into the diet, Monash is a trusted source.

MY GI HEALTH—MICHIGAN/CEDAR SINAI

http://mygihealth.io
Online tools designed to help take control of your GI health by assessing and monitoring symptoms.

NESTLÉ HEALTH SCIENCE'S LOW FODMAP CENTRAL

www.lowFODMAPcentral.com
Nestlé has launched a new website to share resources for patients and health-care professionals about following the low-FODMAP diet.

PATSY CATSOS

http://www.ibsfree.net
Patsy wrote the first book introducing the low-FODMAP diet in the United States (*IBS—Free at Last!)* and leads trainings around the country with Kate Scarlata to educate dietitians.

REFERENCES

Biesiekierski, Jessica R, and Julie Iven. 2015. "Non-coeliac Gluten Sensitivity: Piecing the Puzzle Together," *United European Gastroenterology Journal* 3 (2): 160–65.

Chey, William D. 2016. "Food: The Main Course to Wellness and Illness in Patients with Irritable Bowel Syndrome," *American Journal of Gastroenterology* 111 (3): 366–71.

Chumpitazi, B. P., J. L. Cope, E. B. Hollister, C. M. Tsai, A. R. McMeans, R. A. Luna, James Versalovic, and R. J. Shulman. 2015. "Randomised clinical trial: gut microbiome biomarkers are associated with clinical response to a low FODMAP diet in children with the irritable bowel syndrome." *Alimentary Pharmacology & Therapeutics* 42 (4): 418-427.

"Clinical Trial Demonstrates Success of Low FODMAP diet." 2016. University of Michigan, http://www.uofmhealth.org/news/archive/201605/clinical-trial-demonstrates-success-low-fodmap-diet, accessed July 15, 2016.

Drossman, Douglas A., and William L. Hasler. 2016. "Rome IV—Functional GI Disorders: Disorders of Gut-Brain Interaction," *Gastroenterology* 150 (6): 12–61.

Gibson, Peter R., and Susan J. Shepherd. 2010. "Evidence-Based Dietary Management of Functional Gastrointestinal Symptoms: The FODMAP Approach," *Journal of Gastroenterology and Hepatology* 25 (2): 252–58.

Gibson, P. R., and S. J. Shepherd. 2005. "Personal View: Food for Thought—Western Lifestyle and Susceptibility to Crohn's Disease. The FODMAP Hypothesis," *Alimentary Pharmacology & Therapeutics* 21 (12): 1399–1409.

Halmos, Emma P., Claus T. Christophersen, Anthony R. Bird, Susan J. Shepherd, Peter R. Gibson, and Jane G. Muir. 2015. "Diets that differ in their FODMAP content alter the colonic luminal microenvironment." *Gut* 64: 93–100.

Khan, Muhammad Ali, Salman Nusrat, Muhammad Imran Khan, Ali Nawras, and Klaus Bielefeldt.2015. "Low-FODMAP Diet for Irritable Bowel Syndrome: Is It Ready for Prime Time?" *Digestive Diseases and Sciences* 60 (5): 1169–77.

Monash University App. Food Guide. 2015. The Monash University Low FODMAP Diet App. 2015, http://www.med.monash.edu/cecs/gastro/fodmap/iphone-app.html

Muir, Jane G., and Peter R. Gibson. "2013. The Low FODMAP Diet for Treatment of Irritable Bowel Syndrome and Other Gastrointestinal Disorders," *Gastroenterology & Hepatology* 9 (7): 450.

Rao, Satish Sanku Chander, S. Yu, and A. Fedewa. 2015. "Systematic Review: Dietary Fibre and FODMAP-Restricted Diet in the Management of Constipation and Irritable Bowel Syndrome," *Alimentary Pharmacology & Therapeutics* 41 (12): 1256–70.

Roest, RH de, B. R. Dobbs, B. A. Chapman, B. Batman, L. A. O'Brien, J. A. Leeper, C. R. Hebblethwaite, and R. B. Gearry. 2013. "The Low FODMAP Diet Improves Gastrointestinal Symptoms in Patients with Irritable Bowel Syndrome: A Prospective Study," *International Journal of Clinical Practice* 67 (9): 895–903.

Rome IV Diagnostic Criteria for Functional Gastrointestinal Disorders. 2016. http://theromefoundation.org, accessed August 6, 2016).

Staudacher, Heidi M., Peter M. Irving, Miranda CE Lomer, and Kevin Whelan. 2014. "Mechanisms and Efficacy of Dietary FODMAP Restriction in IBS," *Nature Reviews Gastroenterology & Hepatology* 11 (4): 256–66.

USDA Food Composition Database. https://ndb.nal.usda.gov/.

ACKNOWLEDGMENTS

I want to extend great thanks to my family and friends for their support. I would especially like to thank the following individuals.

Dr. Gerry Mullin, who introduced me to the low-FODMAP diet—thank you for opening up my world to FODMAPs; it has changed my life and allowed me to help many people.

Kate Scarlata, you have been instrumental in letting the world know about FODMAPs, and you have been a generous resource and friend to me.

Kathy Kendall, my first FODMAP mentor and friend.

Thank you to my patients, who have also been some of my best teachers; I continue to learn from all of you every day.

To my husband, Reid, who has spent countless nights in discussion of how many months pregnant I look when I am not following the low-FODMAP diet. You are the most loving source of support, and your endless curiosity is a blessing.

To my mother, Laura Flug, who got me interested in nutrition at a young age. Thank you for cheering me on.

To my father, Robert Flug, who encouraged me to pursue my passions—and to Ellen for her support—thanks for preordering the first copy of this book.

Margie, Kathi, and Carol—I could not have done this without you.

Matt and Alexandra—thank you for your feedback.

Aurora Bell—it has been a pleasure to work with you. Thank you and the rest of the team at Countryman Press for all of your help.

Finally, to Ann Triestman, my wonderful editor, who gave me the opportunity to write this book. I am grateful to you for letting me share this with the world.

INDEX

PHOTO CREDITS